The Calling

May the words on these pages lodge
in your heart and be an inspiration
to you.

Leah's Dad

Jeremiah 17:7-8

Michael L. Straley

ISBN 978-1-0980-8623-7 (paperback)
ISBN 978-1-0980-8624-4 (digital)

Christian Faith Publishing, Inc.
832 Park Avenue
Meadville, PA 16335
www.christianfaithpublishing.com

Printed in the United States of America

To grieving family members and friends who have
lost a loved one to the opioid epidemic

FOREWORD

Tim Fisher, Pastor of Covenant Life Church

> One word frees us of all the weight and pain of life…that word is love.
>
> —Sophocles

I was three steps from the entrance of the hospital, about to make my pastoral rounds, when the phone rang. I glanced down and saw Robin's name. I sat slowly, softly, on the nearby bench as Robin shared of Leah's passing. There are no words in those moments, so I listened. I was transfixed hearing Robin's heartbreak as she recounted the events of the last week of Leah's life.

I pledged my support to Mike and Robin and offered my love; I hung up the phone and remained seated on the bench for several minutes. The breeze gently blowing, I bowed my head and lifted their family to Heaven in a solemn prayer. During the prayer, my remembrance was drawn to the first miracle of Christ at the Cana of Galilee. I concluded the prayer, remained seated, and contemplated Jesus turning water into wine.

It may seem like an odd moment of reflection considering the news I had just received, but somehow it wasn't. I knew when Robin shared of their family's tragedy the story was not over. In fact, I knew that somehow Leah's legacy did not end so abruptly. Her presence may have lifted, but her reach and her influence—those were about to expand.

My mind and imagination fluttered around Jesus taking the ordinary and making it extraordinary.

As you turn these pages you will read of paternal love and the struggles of addiction, and you will feel the heartbreak of a father for his daughter. You will know Leah—but before you do, I want you to know something about my dear friends Mike and Robin. They would consider themselves ordinary. I've heard them say as much so many times. They are not.

They are extraordinary for the same reason Jesus turned water into wine. That first miracle was wrought not to declare the divinity of the man from Nazareth. No, it was because of love. The love of a child for his mother. I've bore witness to the love that Mike and Robin have for Leah. It was love that changed water into wine, and it is love that has transformed Mike and Robin's life from "ordinary" parents to extraordinary caretakers of Leah's Legacy.

Mike and Robin take ordinary items, package them, and in Leah's name reach out to other women in addiction with the legacy of love.

CHAPTER 1

The Call

Valentine's Day—a celebration of love and affection.

I was consumed with choosing a restaurant and food fare for my wife and me on the morning of Wednesday, February 14, 2018, that when my office phone rang at 9:02 a.m., I didn't think anything was out of the ordinary.

I work as the executive director of the Fulton County Medical Center Foundation in McConnellsburg, Pennsylvania. We were in the middle of a major building project on the sprawling ninety-acre campus. The $20 million project had created detours internally and externally.

When the front registration desk name appeared on my office phone, my initial thought was a donor or donor prospect wanted to discuss the Center for Advanced Medicine project.

Teresa's voice on the other end erased those thoughts. She said there were two Pennsylvania State Police officers here to see me.

I said I'd be there, but I had to navigate the internal construction and took the long route from the second floor of the south side of campus to the main lobby, which just had opened. As I traversed the desolate hallways, my mind wandered. *Why do they want to talk with me? Has our home been burglarized? Is there a problem here on campus?*

I quickly made eye contact with the two troopers from about twenty feet. They were in full uniform and weren't smiling. After firm handshakes and introductions, Trooper Jeff Beal asked if we could meet privately.

"Yes, I have an office," I said, "but it's on the other side of campus. I'm sure I can get a vacant conference room nearby."

We walked down the hall and entered Barmont III. The room was cold. I entered first. I heard the door close behind me. The officers stood about three feet from me.

Trooper Beal asked my name again. He asked if my daughter's name was Leah Renee Straley. I said yes, and immediately my thoughts were *What did she do?*

There was a pause that seemed like several minutes, but in reality I guess only a few seconds.

Trooper Beal said: "I regretfully have to tell you that Leah Renee Straley died earlier this morning. We received a call from the Delray Police Department."

"We don't know the details, but this is the toughest part of our job," his partner said. "Take as much time here as you need."

My whole body went numb. I sat down. I asked more questions but don't remember what I asked or remember the answers. I wanted to cry but couldn't. I wanted to throw up but couldn't. I wanted this to be a bad dream, but I knew it wasn't.

Several minutes passed. I said I had to get to Hagerstown, Maryland, to notify my wife, Robin. The officers asked if I had someone to drive me. I said no. They were emphatic that I not drive myself. I was just as emphatic that I would do just that. They asked if they could do anything for me. I nodded no.

They turned left out of the room and went back through the lobby. I turned right then right again. I was in shock because I felt as though my body was floating. I was hoping no one would stop me in the hallways to chat.

About halfway down the second hallway, I felt tears streaming down my checks. I felt a coldness in my body, and my heart literally hurt. I started to quiver. Two left turns and two more hallways, and not a person in sight. It brought me to the stairs and the elevator. I took the stairs. I remember losing my balance a few steps up. I hung onto the railing.

I made my way into the Foundation Department. My one staff member, Chris Boryan, was out that morning. My other staff member, Wendy Farling, walked through the door and stopped at my office door. She saw the distraught look on my face and the tears streaming down my face as I hurriedly put on my coat.

"I gotta go, Wendy. I gotta go. I gotta get to Hagerstown," I said as my voice trailed off.

"What's wrong, Mike? What's wrong?" Wendy pleaded.

As I walked past her and was heading out the door, I said, "We lost her, Wendy. We lost her."

Down the steps I went and to my vehicle. As I started my Chevy Trailblazer, I could barely see to drive from the tears. I grabbed paper napkins from my console and started to wipe endlessly.

The trip to Hagerstown took forever. It wasn't because I got behind tractor trailers navigating the mountainous terrain in the rural setting. Instead, I was fighting physical and emotional barriers that hindered me from driving like a fully capable motorist. Maybe the officers were right. Maybe I should've had someone drive me.

What do I say to Robin? How do I say it? Do I go to her open cubicle at The Herald-Mail newspaper company?

God, give me wisdom and direction on how to deal with this tragedy and how to share the news to my beloved wife.

By now, forty-five minutes of a sixty-minute drive, I had a stack of wet paper napkins beside me. As I turned into the Herald-Mail parking lot, I pulled up to the front curb yet far enough way that it wouldn't impede customers who were coming and going. I texted Robin to meet me outside the building. She immediately responded, "On my way."

She knew I was not surprising her with chocolates or flowers. Call it mother's intuition.

I stood on the sidewalk. From about thirty feet away, she saw the look on my face. I didn't say a word. She read my body language.

"What? What happened? You are scaring me." Those were her initial comments.

I said, "We lost her, Rob. We lost her. We lost Leah."

She collapsed into my arms on the sidewalk as we both hit the pavement. I held her tight and prevented her from injuring herself. We wept on the sidewalk. Longtime employee and then recently-retired Bob Fleenor walked by with a puzzling look on his face as I glanced up. He would later say he knew it was bad news about one of our children.

We returned to the vehicle where we both continued to cry. I had run out of paper napkins. We talked in fits and spurts through our grief, having trouble understanding each other at times. I shared what had transpired earlier that morning with the officers. I had the information they had given me. We dialed the number from my cell phone to the Floridian County Police Department. I asked for Detective Milicchio. I put him on speakerphone.

He shared that Leah's friend, Cathy, whom she was visiting, called 911 on Tuesday night. Cathy's boyfriend, Brian, had overdosed. When the paramedics arrived with the police, Brian was transported to the hospital. Cathy had a warrant out for her arrest, and she was taken into custody. That left our daughter alone in the apartment. When Brian returned to the apartment early the next morning, he found Leah unconscious by the bathroom sink. He tried administering CPR, but she could not be resuscitated. Her body was taken to the nearby medical examiner's office. An autopsy would be performed.

We were grief-stricken and heartbroken.

I walked with Robin back into the newspaper building to get her coat and purse. We were both sobbing. Her coworkers were devastated. Moans and crying abounded, as did long embraces. Work in her department was an afterthought.

We traveled together to Martinsburg, West Virginia, to inform our son, Chris, about his sister's death. He was working a job off-site but was on his way back to the welding fabrication shop. He wanted to know over the phone. We shared the news. He then pulled into the gravel parking lot and saw our puffy red faces. The tears were still streaming down our faces. We all hugged and cried together.

On our way back home, Robin looked at me and, fighting back even more tears, said, "We need to call a local funeral home to make arrangements." I knew her high school classmate had married a funeral director, and I was always impressed with how they handled services.

She called Doug Fiery. He encouraged us to stop by. We did. Less than six hours after the news of our daughter's passing, we were discussing details of her arrangements. He was thoughtful and offered to take care of everything. She would be cremated. He made all the calls and kept us abreast of every detail. We will never forget his caring and compassionate demeanor, along with he and his wife's, Julie, generosity.

What would follow would be the most difficult task I've had to do in my life to date: inform my mom that her beloved granddaughter had passed. We pulled into my parent's driveway. We live beside them in Greencastle, Pennsylvania. We entered the back sliding glass French doors like we had done thousands of times before, but this time was different. My father was sitting in his usual spot in the recliner chair. Mom was in the kitchen. Iszabella, Leah's puppy she had gotten for her high school graduation in 2010, greeted us as well. Mom stopped between the doorway leading from the kitchen to the family room. She saw our faces. She immediately asked what happened. She repeated it several times.

I told her to sit down. She said, "Oh my God, no," even before we broke the news to her. She wept endlessly. We all did. Iszabella, whom we all adopted as now our own, is a Pekingese-Maltese mix. She knew something was wrong and quietly laid down beside me on the couch. We talked and cried. We cried and talked. Mom grabbed a dishcloth and used that as a crying towel. She used it, in fact, for weeks on end.

After about two hours, we finally drove next door to our home. We called our family and closest friends. Shortly thereafter, Denise visited, as did Annette.

Denise and I attended primary and middle school together, and our families had attended the same church. She and her husband, Doug, babysat Leah on many occasions when Robin and I went away on escape weekend vacations. Denise loved Leah like a daughter. Annette's son Seth and Leah graduated together from high school in 2010. She also had attended the same church, and we are very good friends.

That evening, Jeff and Carol visited, as did Glenn and Donna. Jeff and Carol are dear friends of ours. He is such a handyman, and Carol is a good listener. Glenn is a school classmate of mine and very close friend. We have made many sporting trips together. And Donna was Robin's maid of honor and high school classmate.

The day ended with me writing my daughter a love letter. I have done so each night since her passing.

Love letters written to Leah each night

Valentine's Day, 2018—a time for love and affection but not a celebration.

For about a year, Leah wanted to visit Cathy in Florida. We convinced her otherwise. She had first met her in California at a sober living home. She said time and again that Cathy was sober and living a clean life and had encouraged her to visit.

The week before she flew to Florida, Leah relapsed while staying at a sober living home in Ephrata, Pennsylvania. She called and said she had nowhere to go, although the house owner was willing to get her help and back into detox. She declined. Robin, as you will read throughout this book, took it upon herself to help. She traveled two hours to be with our daughter, and they reserved a hotel room. A resident of the sober living home helped Robin move Leah's personal belongings out of the home. Robin also convinced Leah to get help once again. Only this time, it was with state insurance and not mine since she had turned twenty-six.

There is a big difference when you have state insurance versus your own insurance. And she quickly found that out. A driver from the facility that was three hours away picked her up at noon the next day for an all-day excursion. She was not the only passenger, but the first.

Leah was perturbed about the long drive, and then the facility was a "slum" as she described it. It was unlike any other she had been to, and it didn't last but only a few days. She prided herself on being neat and orderly, and her living conditions had to be the same. It was far from it. Filthy living conditions and terrible food prompted her to call home to ask if I would pick her up. Icy winter conditions, especially worse in that part of the state, prompted me to say no.

"Fine," she snapped. "I'll figure something out."

She called less than twelve hours later and said they would be dropping her off at our home, as they made another long run to pick up patients.

On the afternoon of Thursday, February 8, 2018, she arrived, only I didn't see her because I was at work. But I hurriedly left work and stopped at the grocery store to get ingredients to make my homemade lasagna. She loved my lasagna, a dish I learned to make in home economics class in 1981. I got home, and Leah was not here. Disappointed, I thought she was next door with my father and Iszabella.

Nope. Only her luggage was there. It sat in my parent's garage.

She didn't return phone calls or text messages.

I had a knot in my stomach the size of a softball because I knew she was with her so-called "friends" who were users. I didn't sleep well that night. I was on edge at work the next day. When I came home, much to my surprise, she was home and happy. She was cognizant and had no appearance or signs of being under the influence.

She did make the announcement that she was going to Florida to visit Cathy. If she liked it there, she would consider staying. I asked when she was leaving for the Sunshine State and she said the next day.

Whoa.

Her mom French braided her hair and I took a picture of them together.

Robin braiding Leah's hair

Leah was sitting on the carpeted flooring in what we call our Clemson Room, and Robin was happily braiding her hair. In the meantime, she had two suitcases that needed packed, but limited to fifty pounds each. We had fun with that. It was a great night to be together. I slept well that night.

The next day, Saturday, February 10, she spent most of the morning with her grandma, my mom, who asked if my father could ride along to the airport. Sure thing. She couldn't understand why he would want to make that trip because he didn't like long drives. This would be a ninety-minute jaunt, one way.

After hugs with her mom and grandma and niece Jane, my father and I took her to Baltimore/Washington International Airport. She sat in the back seat of the Trailblazer with a Schweppes ginger ale in her hand and headphones affixed to her noggin. She loved listening to all types of music, but for some reason, she wanted to talk on this trip. We had good conversation throughout the ninety-minute trek.

Once at the airline portal, I helped her with her luggage. She checked her bags from the outside baggage area. I watched her from afar and was saddened to see her leave. Since no police officer told me to scurry along, I waited for her to return to where I had parked. She quickly pointed out that she had tipped the baggage handler. I laughed.

She loved getting her picture taken, and I asked if we could get a photo together.

Mike and Leah at airport

Her beautiful smile and face reminded me of how lucky I was to call her my daughter. And as I did countless times before, whether it was dropping her off or picking her up from wherever or whatever, I put my arms around her and looked her in the eye.

I said, "Your biggest fans are at home. We believe in you and love you."

She looked back and genuinely said, "I know, Dad. I love you."

She was smoking a cigarette near the vehicle when I crawled back into the driver's seat. I pushed the button on my side of the door to roll down the passenger's window.

"Hey, Leah!" I exclaimed. "How about a photo with you and Pap Rick?"

She smiled, ducked her head into the window and put her arms around my father.

Leah and Pap Rick at airport

The photo is a keeper. As the window rolled up, I looked at the left facial cheek of my father. A single tear gently rolled down his face. A man of few words, he asked prophetically, "Will we ever see her again?"

I quickly said that she's visiting a friend in Florida. We'll see her again.

Little did I know four days later I would get that call.

She always texted updates about her flight, and this trip was no different. Luggage. Check. Takeoff. Check. Landing. Check. Pickup. Check.

Then on Sunday, she FaceTimed me at 6:00 p.m. She gave Robin and me a virtual tour of her friend's apartment. It looked nice. The weather was great. She was having a good time. Monday's report wasn't so good. Cathy was spending time with Brian, who was moving into the same apartment. Leah wasn't aware of such a move. Tuesday night's call was worse. Both were using drugs, Leah said. Leah was fraught with anxiety. There were too many drugs. She couldn't handle it. Robin told her to look up sober living homes, to start exploring them, and to be strong.

In the weeks and months that followed, Robin said she should've told her to leave the apartment immediately and get to the airport, and she would book a flight to get back home. I doubt she would've heeded that advice.

But to Leah's credit, when her personal belongings were given back to us, including her cellphone, the first page that opened up on the phone was a sober living home she had contacted prior to her passing. More about all of these details in chapter 3.

CHAPTER 2

The Dark Days

Who, what, when, where, why, and how—these are the basic principles of newspaper journalism that were ingrained in me when I was getting my undergraduate degree in communications-journalism.

I had no idea they would apply to my life as a parent who lost a child to a drug overdose. To say Robin and I were numb, heartbroken, confused, and devastated would be an understatement. With little or no sleep, the morning after learning of Leah's passing was just as painful. More phone calls were made and received, as were more visits from friends and family. There was quietness, numbness, and loneliness.

I now have a disdain for being alone in the depths of the quietness in our home, despite seeking quietness within myself. On many occasions my heart races with anxiety and hurt from the grief that toils within my soul.

Robin asked me if I wanted her to call Kevin Simmers to visit us. I said yes, although I had never met the man. He lost his daughter to a drug overdose in 2015 and was in the middle of fulfilling his daughter's dream by building Brooke's House, a sober living home in nearby Hagerstown, Maryland. Robin and Kevin were friends from their high school days. He agreed to visit the following day.

We also had a visit from a couple that had lost their son in a car accident. She was a former coworker with Robin. They were quick to point out they wouldn't be attending any memorial service for our daughter because it was a "trigger." They also mentioned about the importance of "signs from your loved one."

Triggers? I quickly found out about what she was talking about. Grief triggers are those consistent little reminders that keep throwing us back in time. A sight, a sound, a smell, a touch, a person, a place, or a special day can all trigger powerful memories. And out of nowhere, you're ambushed without your consent. It's just how grief triggers are. They're unpredictable, suddenly and unexpectedly catching you off guard. They

THE CALLing

are unrelenting and unavoidable. Just when you thought you were coping with your grief, a trigger reminds you that you're far from the finish line—one that you never cross. It unleashes a flood of mixed feelings on you, putting you on an emotional roller coaster. I experience them every day. They are shared throughout this book.

And signs? After a loved one passes, you're left with a gaping hole in your heart, you may feel lost and alone and angry and sad, while experiencing many other waves of emotions as you go through the mourning process. You feel as if they are gone from your life forever, but the truth is they are always with us. So it makes total sense that sometimes our passed loved ones will try to get messages across to us. They may want to make contact to let you know that they're okay, to give you comfort. It happened shortly after the couple visited us. The next morning when Kevin arrived, I walked out the front door to greet him. I saw a heart shape etched in our mulch by the lamppost. No rabbit or cat could've done that. More signs and details of them are at the end of this chapter and throughout this book.

Kevin, a retired police officer, gave us each a hug. We talked, and he listened. We all cried. He interjected comments at opportune moments. He talked about the struggles of addicts and the science behind those struggles. It piqued my interest. But mainly he was a good listener, and we appreciated that because he knew what we were experiencing. So many people say they know what we're going through, but really they don't unless they have experienced it. I asked about Brooke's House and its progress. He was hesitant to talk about the project. He knew we were hurting. He suggested we talk about that another time. We would, and our family would be forever touched. He stayed for about ninety minutes. It was some of the best therapy Robin and I would receive as a bond was formed between us in an unthinkable way.

Shortly after Kevin left, I started researching the information he had shared about how addiction hijacks the brain. I spent three hours mesmerized reading articles about the brain and its pleasure principle, dopamine, the learning process, tolerance, and compulsion. I was also saddened and angry at myself for not having done the research while Leah was still alive. It would've helped us understand as parents her daily struggles of addiction, instead of simply saying to her, "Why can't you beat this thing."

My beloved coworkers, Wendy and Chris, visited us Friday afternoon. They, too, sat and listened—and cried. They got to know Leah the summer before when she volunteered at Fulton County Medical Center. When I first suggested she volunteer, Leah was hesitant because she didn't know what she would be doing and if she could adequately do the work. She was always lacking self-confidence. Wendy was her supervisor and took Leah under her wing. Their first job together was to travel in Wendy's VW Bug to buy honey for the Medical Center gift shop. Wendy is a mother figure to many of us, and she puts you at ease. Leah bonded well with her. Wendy kept in contact with Leah after her stint at FCMC through snail mail that always included a candy bar. Leah also liked Chris, whom she secretly likened to a teddy bear because of his beard and easygoing personality.

Both Wendy and Chris offered their support in so many ways. They were quick to say they would handle the daily operations of the Foundation and I should focus on my family. The FCMC administrative team also offered its full support as well as the Foundation Board of Directors.

Wendy lost a son in 2009, so she was another person who knew what we were experiencing. Once I returned to work after a month, she was quick to offer some sage advice.

"There will be days when you're driving to work that you'll need to turn around and go home," she said. "There will be days when you'll need to leave work because the grief will be overpowering. People will say stupid things to you, others will ignore you because they won't know what to say. Some days you won't want to see or talk to anyone in the hallway."

I have put a check mark beside each one because what she said has been experienced many times over.

My mom and I attended grief-counseling sessions at a nearby hospice. The counselor was compassionate and gave us support materials. I followed that up by attending a series of weekly hospice group meetings. There were thirteen of us, either as individuals or as couples. I went alone. I shared grief with those who lost daughters, sons, brothers, and wives. The stories were heart-wrenching, and some created triggers for me, including the final session that was designated as a remembrance ceremony. I struggled mightily. I wept in the car when it was over. I cried myself to sleep that night. That happens quite often.

A few days after Leah's passing, there was a heart-shaped red balloon that floated over our house. Robin and her friend Donna had followed it for miles by car. Read about the details at the end of this chapter. It was clearly another sign.

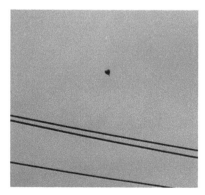

A red heart-shaped balloon—the first sign from Leah

Within a few days of Leah's passing, Robin looked at me and said, "Mike, we need a pastor and a church to hold her remembrance service."

We both knew who we wanted: Pastor Tim Fisher at Covenant Life Church.

We had attended church there for about six years, after leaving another church where we were members for over twenty years. However, we had been away from Covenant Life Church for about two years. Robin was angry with God for not answering her prayers for our kids: Leah's sobriety and our son's, Chris, quest for a productive happy home life of his own. I, too, was angry, faulting the church for not getting to know us better.

Pastor Tim, or PT as he is affectionately called, took the call. Robin had him on speakerphone. His answer didn't waiver: "Of course, I'll do her service."

When we met him a few days later at the church to go over the details, he was seated at the piano on the pulpit singing a song. When our eyes met, it was like reuniting with a long lost friend. In fact, it was just that. PT is in his early forties, multi-talented in music and prose and has a calling from God. His messages are heartfelt and easy to understand. And they stick with you.

We talked for over an hour in his office. He knew about Leah's struggles from previous conversations. Hers wasn't the only one he knew about. There were others from within the congregation.

Addiction doesn't discriminate.

Prior to her death, specifically Friday, February 9, Leah excitedly inquired about March 1. Robin and I were scheduled to meet her in Florida for dinner. I had a speaking engagement at a philanthropy conference; then we were going to spend a few days in West Palm Beach during Major League Baseball spring training. On March 1, we were going to drive a short distance up the coast to meet with her. Leah's assignment was to scout out a restaurant in advance.

Instead, we had her memorial service in Hagerstown, Maryland.

On the morning of Thursday, March 1, 2018, we traveled to BWI airport (another trigger for me) to pick up a friend of Leah's who had flown from Arizona. She wanted to be at the service and spend a few days with us. That night was one of the most difficult times of my life. We stopped at the funeral home to get the urn and then to the church for the memorial service.

There was a display table to the right of us with assorted memorabilia from her twenty-six years. I vaguely glanced at it because the biggest trigger yet today is a photo of my daughter. Yes, we put them in this book, but I'm not to a point in the grieving and healing process where I can look at photos.

The service was scheduled to begin at 6:00 p.m. It got started at 6:30 p.m. because of the line of people offering their condolences. Coworkers of ours, Foundation and FCMC members, Robin's 1982 high school classmates, friends, and relatives, along with Leah's friends and classmates, all waited patiently to hug or share kind words with me; Robin; our son, Chris; and my mom and dad. I sat between my mom and Robin. My handkerchief was soaked by 6:15 p.m. Mom's towel was, too. Friends came from as far as Spartanburg, South Carolina. Some I hadn't seen in five years. It made me cry even more.

I heard the church was packed. I dare not turn around from the first pew to see firsthand because that would have made my situation even worse. PT delivered a wonderful message of hope, promise, and help. He shared testimonials that Robin had collected from two very beautiful ladies in Leah's life.

Jill Kellar (left) and Leah became lifelong friends while in California

The first was from Jill, whom Leah met and befriended and called Jillybean at a sober living facility in California:

Leahbug—

She is/was so beautiful, such a firecracker and soft soul. Clothed in leopard print and Hello Kitty accessories. A smile so contagious, a crinkled nose when she would laugh and the most adorable snort. She truly tried so hard, time and time again. It's such a hard thing to kick and keep at bay. It's a struggle that will never go away. The addiction is cunning, baffling and powerful. I loved Leah. We became sisters in 2013—maybe not by blood, but by God's divine grace and plan. I am forever grateful to him for placing her beautiful face and spirit in my life. Leah helped build my foundation of life. She truly helped me see things in myself that I could never see, and one by loving me even when I was unlovable. She would bake cookies or brownies or walk with me to get ice cream when I was sad. She was the most caring, loving, genuine person I knew. My heart is so heavy. If it wasn't for Leah, I wouldn't be where I am today. There were countless times I wanted to leave and just give up, but Leah was always there to guide me back and help me through some of the most difficult times of my life. So I give a lot of the credit of the foundation of my recovery to your daughter, Leah, and God. God presented an angel in my life to help me stay and begin believing in myself and create a life for myself.

Leah—you were my BEST FRIEND and forever you are my foundation. I love you forever and a day, even after you've left this earth.

Your forever best friend,
Jill

The second was from Amy, owner of a sober living home in California, mentor, and friend of Leah's:

Leahbug, how her smile could light up a room, how lovely her soul. Her fight with the disease of addiction—in times—revealed her true nature, that of a kind, generous of spirit, brave, loving young woman. When Leah was here with us, we saw her struggle with herself, and we saw her overcome. We saw her question herself and ask for help, always with a curiosity that was pure. Without exception, when we would have a new client, who was scared, nervous about being sober or just being in a new environment, Leah would be who I would turn to. She would welcome the newcomer with open arms, having never met her, yet greet her with her endearing smile, soft voice and that gentle way about her. Leah had a positive genius for making others who suffered from her same addiction feel safe, welcomed, and accepted. That's how she got the name "Leahbug"—she was a love bug at heart!

Leah's presence filled a room with comfort, her smile spoke loudly of acceptance, her commitment modeled strength and bravery to those less strong and brave, her love has and will endure in the hearts of all of us who knew her, who know her, and are stronger, braver, more accepting, comforting and better because of her.

As sad as I am today for Leah's family and her friends that she is no longer with us in this physical world, I am so very honored to have known her, to have witnessed her give and grow spiritually, to see her true nature, knowing that is who she is now—free from the sufferings of this physical world—and all that remains is her truest self-kindness, hope, generosity, peace, passion, love and light.

With all my love and blessings,
Amy

I could hear weeping behind me that blended in with the accompaniment of soft keyboard music performed by a church member. The service lasted well past seven o'clock. Afterwards, a fellowship gathering took place downstairs. The church family put it together. Through tragedy, they had gotten to know us.

We were exhausted that night. And the next day, too. And many days and weeks thereafter, as well. So many phone calls to tie up loose ends on the business and personal side of Leah's life.

When we took Leah's friend back to the airport, we wanted her to have a good meal. It was sort of a tradition, albeit a short-lived one, that we would stop at this restaurant off Interstate 695 in Baltimore to enjoy a delicious seafood meal when we're flying in or out of BWI. Leah loved their crab cakes, which are the size of a softball. The restaurant holds over 300 patrons. What are the odds we would be seated at the same table when we last dined there with our daughter? It was both a trigger and a sign. We haven't been back since.

In fact, Robin and I have had to choose several different restaurants now because of the memories they trigger. Leah liked to join us on our birthday and anniversary dinners. We didn't mind because we enjoyed her company and she always liked to dress for the occasion. Her perfume—Viva la Juicy—was divine, I must admit. Restaurants, certain shopping malls, and, yes, holidays, have all changed for us.

Thanksgiving was her favorite holiday, after her birthday on November 10. We no longer have a large meal on Thanksgiving. And we find ourselves doing outreach work, going to the movies or both on that day. Moreover, the days and weeks leading up to Christmas are equally challenging because she loved the hubbub of the holiday season, whether it was shopping or making cookies with her grandma. We've been dark since her passing with no Christmas tree or decorations—and no presents, except for our granddaughter. Celebration is not a word we use anymore.

During the first Christmas in 2018, I was leveled to tears when I saw a coffee commercial that had her name tied to one of her favorite drinks. It's not every day you see the name Leah appear on television. Another sign.

Speaking of beverages, Robin and I shared one a few weeks after her passing when we had to fly to Florida to pick up her belongings. Leah had introduced us to it when we first visited her in California. It was an orange smoothie offered at franchise locations primarily on the West Coast and at airports. We sat at the airport and cried knowing this was going to be an agonizing quick trip while we sipped on this refreshing drink she had introduced us to. It was as if we could still see her smiling and us knowing that she wouldn't be accompanying us, but her personal stuff would soon be home with us. Another sign.

This trip was two weeks after Leah's passing, when we were finally given the go-ahead by the Floridian Police Department to fly to the Sunshine State to pick up her personal belongings. We couldn't do it until Cathy was released on bond and back into her apartment. We didn't want to see her, so she agreed to stay in her room while we collected our daughter's belongings. Call it a business trip, or whatever, but it was a whirlwind twenty-four hours. We flew to Jacksonville, spent the night, drove to the apartment, collected her belongings, recounted in our minds what actually happened that night, sobbed, and kissed the location on the floor where she was found. We then met the detectives in the parking lot who handed us an envelope with more of her personal property and discussed the steps in the investigation. Among the items handed to us was her sobriety ring that we had gotten her a few years prior after she had been clean for nine months. I now wear it adoringly around my neck with a small heart urn pendant. Then it was back to the airport and back home in Pennsylvania. Robin and I had been running on adrenaline for those twenty-four hours, only to be fully drained of energy the next morning that carried over for days.

Through those first few weeks, we didn't eat much. Friends brought food, and we nibbled. We needed to keep hydrated, but we would sit in the living room across from each other and cry. I lost eighteen pounds. And a lot of sleep. Naps in the afternoon were short. My body was still numb. I had a hole in my heart. It's still there.

Also during those first three weeks, I had read in the local newspaper about a lady organizing a Black Balloon Day. It memorializes loved ones each year in March. Vicki and Carrol Rhodes lost their daughter Teri in 2015. Vicki was going to be in town on March 6 tying balloons to the parking meters.

Mike met Vicki Rhodes (right) on Black Balloon Day.
Photo courtesy of Echo Pilot

I called her and agreed to meet her that morning. Another bond in an unfathomable way.

Through this tragedy, I have also collected expressions, signs, and photos. I use these two most often when I speak to groups:

Not until you've lost a child do you know how it feels to be sad everyday...even when you experience joy.

Grief is never something you get over. You don't wake up one morning and say, "I've conquered that; now I'm moving on." It's something that walks beside you every day.

I have written about friends and relatives and how they have helped us in so many ways. There are two groups of people that have played important roles in our lives through this tragedy.

GRASP is an acronym for Grief Recovery After Substance Passing. It's a national group with local chapters. I googled "grief support for parents" on February 15, 2018, and GRASP was one of the first to appear. I clicked on the website and saw Franklin County had a chapter. It is a privately held meeting that requires a phone interview before admittance to a meeting. The Facebook postings are also private. Every day, there are a multitude of postings. It's heart wrenching to see all the beautiful people who have succumbed to this dreaded epidemic. When I called, the lady on the other end was a good listener. I could tell she cared. Lindsay later told me she was glad that I called because of the sadness in my voice. Robin and I attended the monthly meeting less than four weeks after Leah's passing. We were told to bring a photo of our daughter for the photo board. Robin carried the photo. I carried much of the nervousness. There were ten of us that night. The chapter was less than a year old. We were all hurting over the passing of our children or siblings. It was therapeutic yet depressing. I attended two more meetings, then decided I couldn't handle anymore sadness. Two months passed. Robin was still attending the meetings.

She said, "Jerry asks about you at each meeting."

When I decided to go back to the meeting, I was greeted with these words: "Good to see you ol' buddy. Mike, I'm glad you're here."

Jerry has no idea how much those words meant to me—and still do. He and I are mostly the only males in attendance. He makes me smile when I really need it.

The other group of angels—I'll use that term loosely since some could be defined as "characters"—is Robin's high school classmates. There is a core group of them that get together just to, well, get together and hash out old memories, while creating goodwill. They are a good group to fellowship with, and they have our best interests in their hearts. They keep in touch by social media, and every now and then we get together for a meal. They have made donations in Leah's memory.

Days, weeks, and months pass by like the balloon we saw in those first few days after Leah's death. It's still raw. I write her every night. Lots of nights I cry myself to sleep. Sometimes I spray her perfume on the bed in the morning so I can smell it that night. In the beverage cabinet in the garage, there are two full containers—one a flavored water and the other a ginger ale with her name on both. She had purchased them on her last trip to the grocery store. I have the empty ginger ale can she last used on her trip to the airport. About a month after her passing, I found a cigarette that was hers. It's in a plastic bag. A Hello Kitty toy sits in the dash of my vehicle. All the handcrafted orange, purple, and white braided bracelets she's ever made me have been preserved.

And every day, I wear a purple and red ribbon on my attire—red is for substance use disorder and the purple signifies overdose awareness. Sometimes it's a conversation starter as inquiring minds want to know the significance of the ribbon. It's my way of saying she will never be forgotten, letting people know her name and all the good she did for those who she supported in the sober living home environment.

And in my opinion as a former newspaper scribe, that is well worth talking and writing about.

A red and purple ribbon—part of Mike's attire everyday

Signs and Wonders from Robin

A Strand of Hair. On Sunday, February 18, 2018, 10:58 a.m., I was getting dressed. I put on a peach top that I hadn't worn in weeks. As I made my way down the stairs, I felt something pulling at my arm, some kind of tension was present. I looked down and noticed a long brown flowing strand of Leah's hair attached to my arm sleeve. How could this be? Leah had not been home for months and our clothes had not been washed together. I accepted the moment as a lovely sign and bagged the strand of hair for precious safekeeping.

A Heart-Shaped Red Balloon. It was Monday, February 19, 2018, five days after Leah's death on Valentine's Day. I had asked my friend Donna to take me to the local Dress Barn to buy a new pair of black slacks for Leah's memorial service. On the return trip home, we got off the interstate exit and headed north. Once beyond the overpass, I looked to the left where Donna was driving, and something caught my eye out of her window. I couldn't believe it—a balloon had just flown right over the top of our car.

I said to Donna, "Is that a heart-shaped balloon? Is it purple?"

No, it was red. We pulled over on the shoulder of the road, and I took several pictures trying to capture the heart shape as it blew through the air. It was overcast, and the wind was blowing strong, northwest. The balloon was dancing around and going higher and higher. We drove further north tracking the balloon, stopping at every possible pull-off to wait for it to catch up and blow further north. We had lost vision of it for a moment, but then there it was again, going ever higher and higher.

Donna said, "Robin, it's going to your house!"

The balloon veered northwest between an auto dealership and local pizza shop, heading over a housing development that would lead to a field—our house sits right beyond the field. We had no shortcut access to get to my home in time to see it pass over, but I know it did. How could this balloon know to travel three and a half miles in the same direction I am traveling and to the same destination—home? Leah gave me a beautiful gift that day: a sign that she was okay and Christ had found her at that last moment when all was lost and she left us forever.

Charm. I was taking my early morning walk at work on April 5, 2018, doing laps in a venue area; and nearing the end of my walk, I noticed a silver charm lying in front of me. I picked it up, and it said, "Remember, I Love You, Mom" engraved with two interlocking hearts. Thank you, my dear Leah. I needed to hear just one more "I love you" from my girl.

CHAPTER 3

The Investigation

After Leah's passing, grief, anger, hate, questions, and determination set in. Just who is really responsible for Leah's death? Was it Leah because she was an addict that could not control the inner demons of addiction calling her name over and over again, or was it someone else? Someone who had a dealer name and the means to contact, setup the deal, and make the purchase of the lethal, potent concoction that caused my daughter's death.

Leah had left the love and comforts of our home only three days prior on Saturday, February 10, 2018, to move into an apartment with Cathy, someone she had met in a previous year at a sober living home in California. They had so much in common and had stayed in touch. Cathy now lived in her own apartment in her home state of Florida, and through conversations between the two of them, it was decided that Leah would make a fresh start and move down to live with her. Text messages found on Leah's cellphone after her death revealed that Cathy was not clean, and she did let Leah know that up front. Additional text messages found on Leah's cellphone revealed that she would be picking up Leah at the airport and would have a "cap of dope" waiting for her. This would not be a fresh start but the start of life choices that would end three days later.

Leah didn't know any drug dealers in that area. She had just arrived in Florida and was too new to the area. This was not Leah's drug dealer. It was Cathy's or Cathy's boyfriend's dealer. Either way, they became the dealer the moment they decided to get the drugs for someone else.

Day 1, Sunday

On the first day of her new surroundings, Leah had FaceTimed us to show us her new living area and to give us a tour throughout the apartment and outside surroundings. Robin and I remember how the sun was shining so beautifully that day, and she seemed so happy. She loved the warmth of the South and had always hated the cold of the North.

Day 2, Monday

After only one day, there seemed to be trouble brewing. Leah was unaware that Cathy had a boyfriend who was moving into the same apartment. She called home that evening saying she didn't think it was going to work out. We had heard this so many, many times before. She would always run and jump into a plan that was not thought-out properly, and it would usually turn sour within days.

Day 3, Tuesday

After three days, Leah felt alienated by Cathy because she was depending on her for transportation to go here and there to make purchases to set up her room and other items she found that were needed for the house. Only Cathy did not provide the attention that Leah required.

Leah had no car, no knowledge of where anything was and had to depend and rely on Cathy to run errands after work hours.

This night was different. Leah was anxious and had called us around 7:00 p.m. to say that "it's not going to work out." We did not realize it until later, but there was fear in her voice. Too many drugs. Too tempting. She could not say no to so many drugs. Robin told her that if she wanted to stay in Florida, she would need to seek out a sober living home in the area. Why didn't we tell her to just get to the airport and come home? Robin beats herself up mentally for not instructing her to do that. Robin constantly says, "I will never have that moment back."

All were using that night. Conversations with Brian's mother a couple weeks after Leah's death revealed that he and Leah were told by Cathy that the one bag was really strong. Cathy was the only one that did not use from this bag. He ended up overdosing. Narcan was used to revive him, and 911 was called. Emergency personnel came and worked on him. Leah was answering police questions. But they had found an active warrant out for Cathy for petty theft, and she was taken outside of the apartment where she was arrested and taken away. Cathy would be searched later while in custody when cocaine would be found in her possession. Brian was taken to the hospital. That left Leah alone in the apartment.

Due to the Good Samaritan law, Leah was not taken into custody. We could not understand why they did not arrest Leah, but due to this law as long as an individual is reporting an overdose and seeking medical attention for someone, no arrests can be made for possession of a controlled substance unless there's a good reason to do so—such as an active warrant. All visible drug items were removed by officers on the scene, including three crack pipes and a syringe, which were disposed of. Thinking back on it now, we suspect drugs were hidden before emergency and police personnel arrived at the scene, leaving Leah vulnerable in the hours that followed. Police said they had no reason to arrest Leah because body cams showed Leah cooperating and answering their questions and walking around the apartment. She showed no signs of being in trouble, physically.

It's unclear what happened during the early hours leading up to the next morning. Robin knows that Leah reached out and spoke to a sober living home in that area around 11:00 p.m. that night and held a five-minute conversation with someone. Robin had turned her cellphone off like she does each night. An act, Robin says, she will regret for the rest of her life, although phone records revealed that Leah did not try to call her mom. Robin turned her phone on when she awoke the next morning to the arrival of a text message from Leah saying that the boyfriend had overdosed and the police were in the apartment. Robin replied back—no response. Phone records show there was activity on her phone until after 3:00 a.m.

Wednesday, February 14, 2018

Brian left the hospital early that morning on Valentine's Day around 4:30 a.m. He came home to find Leah on the floor of the apartment. She was gone. Forever. Overdosed. No one was there to save Leah.

Who is to blame? Police said she was cooperating and showed no signs of overdose, but Leah had to have used again after everyone left. Maybe she was scared. Maybe her hope was gone.

She had died not long before she was found.

If there was a needle, it may have been confiscated by someone because detectives did not find any when her body was moved. We don't really know what happened except her autopsy showed a small amount of Fentanyl in her system. A very, very small amount can kill you. Investigators said that officers located several plastic bottle caps with suspected narcotic residue and cotton. There were also several plastic baggies and orange syringe caps. No syringe or pipes were located that night.

We flew down two weeks later to collect Leah's belongings from the apartment. Cathy found out about Leah a week later when she was released from jail. He left us into the apartment while Cathy remained in a closed bedroom. At the time, we did not want to speak to her. We did not want to see her. We painfully gathered and packed Leah's belonging. Before we left, Robin asked him where Leah was found. Brian showed us. Robin knelt down and, with grieving sobs and tears falling from her eyes, kissed the floor where she had been found only days prior. We met with Detectives Gio Milicchio and Michael Shiner in the apartment complex parking lot where we were handed Leah's cellphone. Detective Milicchio said he could not find anything on her phone regarding a drug purchase. He also said that "if Leah had asked for help, or appeared that she was in danger, they would have taken her for further medical treatment."

While in the parking lot, we also ran into the apartment manager, who Robin had spoken with several times by phone to gain access to the apartment to get Leah's personal belongings. The apartment manager promised to return our call, but never did, leaving us to wonder if we would ever get Leah's belongings returned to us. Once Robin realized who she was, she spoke out loudly and voiced her disapproval on how she mishandled the situation, leaving grieving parents in the dark. The apartment manager had a non-compassionate attitude as she jumped in her golf cart and abruptly drove off. It was back to the airport with heavy hearts and feeling of disbelief, remorsefulness, and anger. The next day at home, Robin and I felt so empty. We had been running on adrenalin for the previous forty-eight hours that when we awoke that Friday morning, we were both physically and mentally worn out.

A couple more days passed. Robin turned on Leah's phone to see a voicemail from Detective Mark Lucas. He was doing a follow-up with Leah to see how things were going from Brian's drug overdose. After listening to his message, Robin realized that he did not know that Leah had died that night. Robin called Detective Lucas and explained that he had left a message for Leah Straley and that she was her mother. Robin proceeded to tell him that Leah had died that night. He was shocked and sincerely gave his condolences. This would be the detective that would try his best in every way possible, and as polite as possible, to answer all our questions and concerns into the investigation of Leah's death.

Robin started to Google search drug overdose with arrest and had found a story written by Krista Torralva in the Orlando Sentinel, based in Florida, about Kristy Dyroff, a mother who lost her son, Wesley Greer, to a fentanyl overdose. Wesley had been clean and sober for over a year and was about to start a new job managing rental properties, and a wedding was in his future plans. On August 18, 2015, Wesley ordered heroin from a drug dealer using a social media networking website. Kristy found her son dead the very next day.

Robin immediately sent an e-mail to the reporter, and she sent her e-mail to Kristy. Within an hour, Robin received a phone call from her. She explained her son's death and the investigation. Then she uttered the phrase "drug-induced homicide" and that charges could be brought against a drug dealer if evidence could be found to warrant an investigation. Kristy and Robin's conversation lasted well over an hour. Kristy also invited Robin to a closed Facebook group with over one thousand members (mainly grieving mothers) who had lost their child to a drug overdose or poisoning. The focus is mothers seeking justice on their children's behalf. This Facebook group was also an outlet for mothers to tell their child's story, how they died and speak openly about their grief and gaining support from other grieving mothers.

Because of these strong-willed, determined grieving mothers they are making new laws and bringing drug dealers to trial seeking justice for their loved ones.

- Wesley Greer, 29, Brunswick, Georgia, died August 19, 2015 (fentanyl poisoning). Drug dealer convicted and sentenced to 20 years in federal prison. Wesley is the son of Kristy Dyroff.
- Sydney Schergen, 18, Chicago, Illinois, died May 31, 2015 (Ecstasy toxicity). Two dealers convicted of drug induced homicide. Sydney is the daughter of Terry Almanza.
- Kyle Dodds, 24, Miami, Florida, died September 26, 2016 (mixture of fentanyl, carfentanil, and synthetics). Kyle's addiction stemmed from a prescription of OxiContin due to a sport injury. Kyle is the son of Cindy Dodds.
- Rhett Dwyer, 21, Jacksonville, Florida, died May 12, 2017. Trial pending. Rhett is the son of Bonny Batchelor-Dwyer.

Robin was told to push our investigator, be persistent, but always be polite. Kristy, along with others, helped Robin compile and ask the below questions over a series of weeks.

Here are Robin's conversations with Detective Lucas that were logged between March 25–April 24, 2018. "Probable cause" is spoken a lot as well as "You must have evidence." Robin worked tirelessly to begin an investigation and ultimately bring justice to those involved with the death of our daughter. Unfortunately, road blocks prevailed.

Robin's questions are in roman; Detective Lucas's answers are in italics:

Social Media:

- Have you preserved all of Leah's, Cathy's, and Brian's social media accounts? Communication is constantly done through Messenger.
    No, we have no probable cause to take such action so a judge would not allow that.
- Did you investigate or find anything on Leah's phone?

The detective reviewed the content in the phone and could not identify any local phone numbers or messages which would provide the identity of a possible drug dealer in the area.

- When Cathy was taken into custody, was her phone searched for buying and picking up drugs from her dealer or does that apply under the Good Samaritan law that you can't search her phone?

    It was not searched, that I'm aware of. It is not covered under the Good Samaritan Act, but it is covered under the Fourth Amendment of the US Constitution which provides people to be secure in their persons, houses, papers, and effects against unreasonable searches and seizures. There just wasn't probable cause to conduct such a search.

- Since Cathy was arrested due to an outstanding warrant, wouldn't that supersede the Good Samaritan law? Have you reached out to the DEA (Drug Enforcement Administration)?

    I am in contact with DEA on every overdose that occurs in that Florida town. I enter all numbers associated with each overdose hoping to make a connection to a seller. In this case, no connection was made in our or the DEA's database.

Leah's Phone:

Robin found several text message conversation trails between Leah and Cathy in regards to introducing Leah to her dealer, getting the drugs and picking them up for Leah. Cathy is the middleman because Leah did not know a dealer and relied on her to get them, buy them, and bring them back for her. Cathy had the transportation, too. Leah did not.

- Please read this article—https://www.thelawman.net/Drug-Offenses/Florida-Drug-Induced-Homicide-Laws.shtml

    Interesting article, thank you for sharing. If we can obtain evidence that is admissible in court, in that county, then charges can be brought against someone involved in a death cause by heroin use. Key factors here are evidence and admissible. As per our conversation on the phone, it has been done one time in that county in federal court. In Leah's case, we are nowhere near that, but I am always open to review new evidence that we obtain.

- Was Leah's phone dumped and put on a hard drive for the investigation?

    No. Since there was no dealer information on the phone, standard procedure is to return the phone to the family.

- Detective Milicchio, you said there was nothing on her phone regarding dealer conversations. However, text conversations between Cathy and Leah clearly spell out that her friend got, bought, and transported the drugs back to Leah.

  I understand your point here, and I would use those messages to try and get details from her "friend." But remember that she has a right to remain silent, so unless she wants to cooperate with us, we'll never get the full story of what happened. I understand how emotional it must be to read those text messages, but for court presentation, so much more is needed. Please try to recall the conversation we had on the phone... I can explain it again if you ever want to call me to discuss.

Cathy:

- Can you pick her up for questioning?

  No. If I ever get the chance to interview, I will. But remember, she has a right to remain silent.
- She is connected to Leah's death because she went and got and brought the drugs for her. There have been other overdoses that Cathy has been involved in before and after Leah's death. How many more victims will Cathy take down? How many more need to die before this piece of trash is brought in and hit hard with her actions that led to Leah's death. She is definitely on the hook for delivering the drugs.

  She and Leah were both fighting a serious drug addiction. Her friend had the means to obtain the drugs, and if our investigation provides court-admissible evidence, I will be the first in line to charge Cathy.

Brian:

- Can you ping his phone to find him to bring him in for questioning?

  No, there is no probable cause to conduct such action, and a judge would not approve that. I will interview him if I ever get the chance. Just remember that he too has a right to remain silent.

Brian's Mother:

- Who is she, and what does she know? She seems to know Cathy and also about Leah's death. She's also talking about her son who overdosed by the hands of his girlfriend (based on a Facebook post).

Can you reach out to her to find out what she knows or where to find her son? Maybe she could help with bearing down on Leah's "friend."

I don't know who this woman is, but I have tried to contact her with the two numbers we have for her. Both numbers are not current. If you hear from her and she would be willing to talk to me, that would be great.

- I have messaged his mother but no response. She is not a frequent user of Facebook. I will try again.
  I have called and texted her but have had no return calls or texts from her.

Additional Conversations:

- When Brian came back and found Leah dead and since he had overdosed the night prior, don't you think a search warrant should had been sought for his phone or to preserve his social media? But I'm not sure if he has one.
  That would be a great option if the law allowed for it. In this case, we do not have probable cause to conduct such a search.
- He was the supplier, and from what I understand, it was through his dealer that drugs were purchased and Cathy picked up and brought back to Leah and she died. I know a lot of this is speculation and hoping that these two individuals would tell me the truth, but they have no reason to.
  Agree. Speculation and circumstances would suggest that, but we still need court admissible evidence.
- Can you tell me what drugs were found and confiscated when Leah was found, or was everything cleaned up? I feel he had plenty to hide, cleaned up the scene before emergency and law enforcement arrived, and now he's off the map.
  There were three types of prescription pills (in their bottles) found which were entered into evidence.
- Section 301.2 (copied from a law enforcement website page) Search, Collection, Preservation and Process of Evidence states the following:

Every coroner and every law enforcement officer will probably, at one time or another have to do one or more of the following activities related to physical evidence:

o   Search for evidence
o   Collect evidence

o   Preserve evidence

o   Process evidence for examination

Thus, it is very important that every coroner and every law enforcement officer understand the importance of physical evidence as it relates to the successful resolution of a criminal case and the successful prosecution of the offender.

Agree with this, and I do understand the importance of physical evidence, not circumstantial evidence but actual physical evidence, which is what we are lacking at this point.

- I am told by another law enforcement officer that you do NOT need probable cause to preserve a social media account. Only connection needed is an official investigation. Probable cause is required to compel the disclosure of the stored contents of any account (to include Brian, Cathy, and Leah), which may include messages, photos, videos, timeline posts, and location information. The preservation freezes the content in the event page is deactivated, content deleted, or settings edited to stricter guidelines.

That officer might be correct as I have heard different answers myself. But please remember that we have no evidence to suggest that they used Facebook to communicate with any dealers, so obtaining a search warrant would not be option.

- Here is the Facebook link to request disclosure for preservation only—
  o   https://www.facebook.com/records/login/
  o   http://blog.legalsolutions.thomsonreuters.com/law-and-techology/facebook-and-police-warrants-can-they-really-do-that/

I'm sure you dread seeing yet another email from me. I just can't give it up and let it go! I know it was Leah's choice, but she had no clue what she was taking, and she put her trust in these two individuals.

I am a detective doing my job, been so for 23 years. I don't mind the emails as I know you're dealing with a lot of grief.

Cathy's Hearing Regarding Cocaine Possession the Night of Brian's Overdose When She Was Arrested:

- I found her court hearing info. I was told to reach out to the prosecutor Michael Delsontro regarding this case to see if any of my evidence could be admitted or any info you are gathering could be submitted to help with the cocaine possession charge against her. States Attorney Advocate Louie Rodriguez said you would need to file an official police report of the evidence I have provided and/

or gathered (screenshots, conversations with the boyfriend's mother and her son, etc.). Does this make sense to you, or would everything still be in limbo waiting to see if his mother or he will talk?

He and his mother have nothing to do with the possession of cocaine charge, so it would not matter.

- I got the feeling that nothing could be done or added to this case number for cocaine possession unless there is a new police report. Could this current hearing be postponed by prosecutor if new evidence was found and that an investigation is ongoing?

    No. Again, that charge has nothing to do with the death investigation.

- Could another charge be added to the current one?

    No, they are unrelated.

- I heard that if this current hearing proceeds and Cathy gets away with it, we cannot not use it for a new charge.

    Again, that possession of cocaine charge has no bearing on the death investigation. It can be mentioned at sentencing if the judge wants to hear from other people, but that's about it.

- Detective—I'm seeking a DRUG-INDUCED HOMICIDE charge against Cathy in hopes that she will give up the dealer. After all, she purchased, transported, and provided the drugs to Leah which led to her death. Of course, I have no proof of that right now, but it's all on Cathy's phone, and I feel confident that Brian knows.

    He may. We'll need his cooperation for sure which he does not have to give.

- Could some of these be an option if certain things fall into play?

    1. Subpoena Cathy's phone and Facebook Messenger records to find conversations of drug buy

        Subpoenas would only give us numbers, not content of messages. We would need a search warrant for that which we do not have probable cause for.

    2. Contact Brian through his mother in hopes of her son's cooperation. He knows what went down that night—who the dealer was and who went and got the drugs. He was probably with her when they were purchased.

        Great idea, which I do on all my investigations. The mother and son to date have not called me or answered any of my calls. It's their choice to cooperate with law enforcement. I have tried to reach her every day since you gave me her number.

    3. Could prosecution give him immunity to testify against Cathy if he cooperates?

        The prosecution could give immunity, but that would be up to the prosecutor's office. I do not have that authority.

4. Subpoena his medical records from overdose to see if toxicology matches up with Leah's medical examiner's toxicology reports, once available

   Not an option. Those are very private. We would need to make a case on physical evidence, not circumstantial evidence.

5. Do you reach out to the prosecutor?

   I have not contacted a prosecutor as I have not had a reason to yet.

6. I will leave you alone for a while to do your work. Please get back to me if you have anything to report. I know I have a lot of questions and some you had answered already, but I just need to put my thoughts down to make sure I cover everything.

   No problem. Please remember that I would like to make an arrest as such, if not more, than you do. If I get court-admissible evidence to prove such a charge, I will definitely contact the prosecutor to discuss.

As parents, we wrote to the judge regarding Cathy. We believe the letter was never read and it wasn't admissible to the cocaine possession, so it was all for naught.

Robin had no more conversation with Detective Lucas because we had no evidence to even try to get a search warrant. Brian would hang up on Robin when she called, and eventually he disconnected his phone. Cathy disconnected her phone and moved too. Robin has since seen her on Facebook and in California for treatment. We have pretty much put that behind us. We continue to grieve and focus only on our daughter and what we can do in her memory.

Robin said she remembers a time when she and Leah were discussing her friends who have addiction problems and how she blamed them, even hated them for Leah's addiction. During one conflict when a friend was on her way to our house to deliver drugs to Leah, there was a struggle where Robin took Leah's phone from her and called this friend, screaming at the top of her lungs that if she placed one foot on our property, she would shoot her dead. That's just how far a parent will go to save their child. We just wanted to save her.

Leah told Robin days later, "Mom, you have to realize that she's in her own addiction just like I am. It's my problem, not yours."

Robin had always helped Leah in finding treatment, finding a rehab facility, finding a sober living home, finding doctors and therapists, and mapped out public transportation.

Anything and everything she would research in hopes that she would find the answers and find the right treatment to try to help fix Leah, but she had to come to terms that she could not fix Leah.

It was up to Leah, and now it was too late.

I Cry

Michael L. Straley

Another ending to another day.
I feel empty. I am not OK.
I cry because I didn't get a chance to say goodbye.
Day after day, week after week, month after month. An endless empty feeling.
There is no healing.
I cry because I didn't get a chance to say goodbye.
You are in my heart, you are in my soul.
You are forever loved as I grow old.
I cry because I didn't get a chance to say goodbye.
My mind wanders. My heart aches.
Life is now more difficult because of the mistakes.
I cry because I didn't get a chance to say goodbye.
People say move on, it's probably better this way or I know how you feel. No you don't because every day it's real.
I cry because I didn't get a chance to say goodbye.
I never thought at age 26 you would die.
I cry because I didn't get a chance to say goodbye!

Blog posted on Dec. 25, 2019

CHAPTER 4

Addiction Education 101

Addiction does not discriminate.

As I wrote in chapter 2, Robin and I were oblivious to the stronghold drug addiction had on our daughter. She was not alone.

According to the Centers for Disease Control and Prevention (CDC), oxycodone, hydrocodone, heroin, and fentanyl have killed more than 400,000 Americans since the turn of the century, a quarter of whom have died from fentanyl in just the last six years.

The opioid epidemic has been a major driver of declining life expectancy for Americans. And while every community seems to be experiencing this crisis differently, there seems to be a trend of how pills, heroin, and fentanyl have gutted society and uprooted our families. CDC reports that from 2000 to 2011, more than 12 billion oxycodone and hydrocodone pills were shipped to pharmacies across the country and that prescription pills were the primary killers of opioid users throughout much of the nation. In 2011, pill deaths had risen to 16,000 annually, more than three times the number from a decade before.

After the Drug Enforcement Administration (DEA) started cracking down on prescription opioids, addicts hit the streets looking to make purchases. It meant less time raiding bathroom cabinets and medicine drawers, and more time stealing from parents, families, and friends to get money to make these purchases. If it wasn't money being stolen, it would be tangible items such as laptop computers, jewelry, and even prized possessions.

While the first wave of the opioid epidemic was addiction and deaths from prescription pills, the second wave was made up of heroin. According to the CDC, from 2011 to 2014, as deaths from prescription pills plateaued, deaths from heroin more than doubled. Although it never reached the death rate that of prescription pills, it served as a conduit into the illegal market for many of those already addicted to pills. Once again, street buyers would find an even deadlier drug awaiting them: fentanyl.

Fentanyl has been used in this country for decades, mostly as a legally prescribed medicine. It is an opioid drug fifty times more powerful than heroin. Starting in 2013, it started flowing into the United States illegally in large quantities, primarily from China. Drug pushers started mixing it with heroin. From 2013 to 2017, according to the CDC, fentanyl overdose deaths rose tenfold to almost 29,000.

First responders in every community are overwhelmed with fentanyl overdoses. In 2018, for example, 621 out of every 100,000 EMS calls in this country resulted in naloxone being administered, according to the National EMS Information System.

On February 14, 2018, EMTs were called to an apartment in a small beach town in Florida. They were able to save one of the occupants through naloxone—that person was not our daughter, who was later found dead in the same apartment. No needle marks. No oral ingestion. Autopsy results showed death by absorption.

The word *addiction* is derived from a Latin term for "enslaved by" or "bound to." Anyone who has struggled to overcome an addiction—or has tried to help someone else to do so—understands why.

Addiction exerts a long and powerful influence on the brain that manifests in three distinct ways: craving for the object of addiction, loss of control over its use, and continuing involvement with it despite adverse consequences.

Leah's addiction started in her midteen years when she started experimenting with marijuana. It was readily available at school—in the parking lot and during the school day, she said to me in the summer of 2017. Away from home, she was smoking joints. At home and around family members, she was a cigarette smoker. It took us as parents a few weeks to figure out she was smoking marijuana. Her behavior patterns matched those signs of use you read about.

As I reflect, it shouldn't have come as a surprise marijuana was used at the outset of her addiction. There is ample evidence that early initiation of drug use primes the brain for enhanced later responses to other drugs. Marijuana use is correlated with alcohol and cigarette use, as well as illegal drugs like cocaine, methamphetamine, and heroin. This does not mean that everyone who uses marijuana will transition to using heroin or other drugs, but it does mean that people who use marijuana also consume more illegal drugs than people who do not use marijuana, according to National Survey on Drug Use and Health by US Department of Health and Human Services. Moreover, people who are addicted to marijuana are three times more likely to be addicted to heroin, according to the CDC.

The aggressive commercialization of marijuana and the push to legalize it as a recreational drug for adults by states for tax benefits is now rampant and damaging to the health of our public, especially now with the eye-catching packaging featuring cookies in gourmet flavors or assorted mouth-watering chocolates. These treats are enough to tempt anyone, especially impressionable adolescents.

Marijuana use during adolescence has been linked to mental health issues later in life. A 2019 meta-analysis of more than 23,000 participants published in the medical journal *JAMA Psychiatry* found that individuals who began using marijuana at least weekly before the age of eighteen were almost 40 percent more likely to develop depression in adulthood. This early regular usage also significantly increased the likelihood of suicidal behavior in later years.

The high levels of THC (tetrahydrocannabinol), the main psychoactive compound in marijuana that gives the high sensation, found in today's marijuana-based products could have something to do with the rise in emergency department visits in states that have legalized marijuana. The Alcohol and Drug Abuse Institute at the University of Washington found that today's marijuana "crystals" sold in legal marketplaces in Seattle contained a maximum of 79 percent THC, marijuana "sauces" were at 83 percent, and certain candies were tested at 85 percent. In contrast, the average THC content of marijuana tested in 1980 was just 1.2 percent.

Scores of young people, like Leah, didn't wait until they reached the legal age to smoke cigarettes or drink alcohol. What's to say it wouldn't be any different for marijuana.

After Leah's passing, we teamed with Vicki and Carrol Rhodes to carry out a public awareness campaign on the opioid epidemic in our small rural community. Held in conjunction with the National Overdose Awareness Day in late August, we put together a one-night event at a local park. It featured agencies and organizations that offer support in prevention, treatment, and recovery services. There was music, food, naloxone training and distribution, activities for children, and a featured speaker. The first year drew nearly 200 guests, the second year only about a fourth of that number.

When I said we were oblivious to her struggles until it was too late, it simply means this: yes, we knew she had an addiction problem, but we didn't know the daily struggles she experienced in trying to overcome this disease. It was not as easy as "Why can't you beat this thing?"

Opioid tolerance, dependence, and addiction are all manifestations of brain changes resulting from chronic opioid abuse. The opioid abuser's struggle for recovery is in great part a struggle to overcome the effects of these changes.

According to the *Harvard Mental Health Letter* and *Overcoming Addiction: Paths Toward Recovery*, a special health report published by Harvard Health Publications, the brain registers all pleasures in the same way, whether they originate with a psycho-active drug, a monetary reward, a sexual encounter, or a satisfying meal. In the brain, pleasure has a distinct signature: the release of the neurotransmitter dopamine in a cluster of nerve cells lying underneath the cerebral cortex. Dopamine release in these cells is so consistently tied with pleasure that neuroscientists refer to the region as the brain's pleasure center.

All drugs of abuse, from nicotine to heroin, cause a particularly powerful surge of dopamine in these cells. The likelihood that the use of a drug or participation in a rewarding activity will lead to addiction is directly linked to the speed with which it promotes dopamine release, the intensity of that release, and the reliability of that release.

Even taking the same drug through different methods of administration can influence how likely it is to lead to addiction. Smoking a drug or injecting it intravenously, as opposed to swallowing it as a pill, for example, generally produces a faster, stronger dopamine signal and is more likely to lead to drug misuse.

Dopamine not only contributes to the experience of pleasure, but also plays a role in learning and memory—two key elements in the transition from liking something to becoming addicted to it. Repeated exposure to an addictive substance or behavior causes nerve cells in the nucleus accumbens and the prefrontal cortex (the area of the brain involved in planning and executing tasks) to communicate in a way that couples liking something with wanting it, in turn driving us to go after it. That is, this process motivates us to take action to seek out the source of pleasure.

According to the current theory about addiction, dopamine interacts with another neurotransmitter, glutamate, to take over the brain's system of reward-related learning. This system has an important role in sustaining life because it links activities needed for human survival (such as eating and sex) with pleasure and reward.

The reward circuit in the brain includes areas involved with motivation and memory as well as with pleasure. Addictive substances and behaviors stimulate the same circuit—and then overload it.

Over time, the brain adapts in a way that actually makes the sought-after substance or activity less pleasurable. In nature, rewards usually come only with time and effort. Addictive drugs and behaviors provide a shortcut, flooding the brain with dopamine and other neurotransmitters. Our brains do not have an easy way to withstand the onslaught. Addictive drugs, for example, can release two to ten times the amount of dopamine that natural rewards do, and they do it more quickly and more reliably. In a person who becomes addicted, brain receptors become overwhelmed. The brain responds by producing less dopamine or eliminating dopamine receptors—an adaptation similar to turning the volume down on a loudspeaker when noise becomes too loud. As a result of these adaptations, dopamine has less impact on the brain's reward center. People who develop an addiction typically find that, in time, the desired substance no longer gives them as much pleasure. They have to take more of it to obtain the same dopamine "high" because their brains have adapted—an effect known as tolerance.

At this point, compulsion takes over. The pleasure associated with an addictive drug or behavior subsides—and yet the memory of the desired effect and the need to recreate it (the wanting) persists. It's as though the normal machinery of motivation is no longer functioning.

These memories help create a conditioned response—intense craving—whenever the person encounters those environmental cues. Cravings contribute not only to addiction but to relapse after a hard-won sobriety. A person addicted to heroin may be in danger of relapse when he sees a hypodermic needle, for example, while another person might start to drink again after seeing a bottle of whiskey. Conditioned learning helps explain why people who develop an addiction risk relapse even after years of abstinence.

Leah relapsed on several occasions. We didn't understand the *why*. We didn't take the time to know the scientific explanation. We just wanted to "fix" Leah. Ultimately, though, it was Leah who had to do the "fixing" and she tried. God knows she fought valiantly.

My Collection of Signs and Expressions

- If you simply cannot understand why someone is grieving so much for so long, then consider yourself fortunate that you don't understand.
- I had my own notion of grief. I thought it was the sad time that followed the death of someone you love. And you had to push through it to get to the other side. But I'm learning there is no pushing through. But rather, there is absorption, adjustment, and acceptance. And grief is not something you complete, but rather you endure. Grief is not a task to finish and then move on but an element of yourself. It's an alteration of your being. It's a new way of seeing and a new definition of self.
- My mind still talks to you and my heart still looks for you. But my soul knows you're at peace.
- But in all the sadness, when you feel like your heart is empty and lacking, you've got to remember that grief isn't the absence of love. Grief is the proof that love is still there.
- On that day, everything changed. Since that day, nothing has or will ever be the same again.
- The years 2010–2020—the decade we lost half a million Americans to the opioid crisis.

Dad's Love

Author Unknown

People don't always see the tears a DAD cries,
His heart is broken too when his beloved child dies.
He tries to hold it together and tries to be strong,
Even though his whole world's gone wrong.
He holds on to her as her tears fall,
Comforts her throughout it all.
He goes through his day doing what he's supposed to do,
But a piece of his heart has been ripped away too.
So when he's alone he lets out his pain,
And his tears come down like pouring rain.
His world has crashed in all around him,
All that was bright has gone completely dim.
He searches for answers but none are to be found.
Who offers to help a DAD up when he's hit the ground.
He smiles through his fears,
Struggles trying to hold in his tears,
But what you see on the outside is not always real.
Men don't always show how they really feel.
He feels he has to be strong for the others,
But DADS hurt too, not just the mothers.

CHAPTER 5

Leahbug

When Robin and I first learned that Leah was using drugs, we were shocked, angry and embarrassed—our daughter could not be one of those persons—you know the kind that people whisper about, the type that will bring shame to the family.

We tried hiding it for years, while helping our daughter get treatment. There were good days, good weeks, and good months. There were battles, struggles, and scars for everyone. There were relapses, not only for our beautiful daughter but for us as parents. It was a rollercoaster ride for all who loved this vibrant young lady.

Leah succumbed to peer pressure in her early teens. She dealt with being accepted and what she perceived as failures in life. It led to drugs. I first looked at it as a habit. Unbeknownst to me, it was a disease. And it's now an epidemic.

As her dad, I felt betrayed at first, then guilt. There was always anger. Anger channeled to why Leah would always give in to her so-called friends and not heed our parental advice. It was crushing at times.

When my cell phone would ring at work, I hesitated to answer it because I had been conditioned over the years that it was bad news from Robin. You see, Robin has always been the go-to person for our children. In Leah's case, she was her rock.

When Robin and I attended a mandatory parents retreat at an upstate rehab center that Leah was enrolled in, there were the usual nuggets of information that I had heard so many times before. But near the end of the session, one of the parents made a plea to our group: "NEVER GIVE UP ON YOUR CHILDREN. No matter the torment, no matter the heartache, NEVER GIVE UP." He had lost a daughter to drug addiction. Another one of his children was in rehab.

Those words lodged in my heart, and I never forgot them. Yet, there was always this rollercoaster ride. College scholarship, dean's list, quit. Job, income, quit. Drug-free, drug use, detox, rehab, sober living. Repeated almost a dozen times. Yet we loved her for who she was, not what she was.

You see, anyone who has lost a loved one through drugs knows that society treats that death in a much different manner than a death from any other cause. There is the unspoken feeling that the individual who succumbed to drugs must have somehow been less than a good person. And for the persons who have survived, surely, they too must have somehow been a failure for "letting this occur."

As parents, we could never see the side of Leah that many—and I mean a lot—of her peers in rehab saw. Many of those tributes were shared at her memorial service and appear on her foundation website (www. leahslegacy.net) and in this book. She was an inspiration to so many who were guided and helped by our beautiful daughter.

I am here to tell you that Leah was loved by many and none any more than her parents and grandma and pap.

As I mentioned before, I always told her, including the last time we were together when I took her to the airport, that *we believed in her, we loved her,* and that *her biggest fans were at home.* She always smiled and said, "I know dad. And I love you for that."

She is now safe and doesn't have to struggle with this hellish disease. I will *always be her biggest fan,* and she will *always be in my heart.*

Born on Sunday, November 10, 1991, at 5:50 a.m., she weighed five pounds, nine and a half ounces. So tiny that I was afraid to pick her up. Once I did, however, in that hospital room, I didn't want to put her down. When she opened her eyes, she made immediate contact with mine.

A new proud dad holding his newborn baby girl

I called her "sweetness" as a baby. She had her mom's great looks; and her big brother, Chris, was very protective of her. He was nine years older than Leah.

Big brother, Chris, holding his little sister

Her mom and I would sing the theme song to *Hawaii Five-O* while we bathed her in the small tub. She would smile and later have the cutest deep belly laugh and grin without a tooth in her mouth.

On one occasion, when she started eating table food, we cut up a hot dog in tiny pieces; and she was so excited to eat it that she started choking. I picked her up and firmly gave her back blows just like my first aid training had taught. The wiener was dislodged. She didn't like hot dogs for quite a while after that incident.

As she grew, so did her good looks and personality. She would go for walks with her Pap Rick.

She would follow behind him as he surveyed his potato fields on a daily basis. She loved to wear her little purple Amish dress. She would serve me make-believe tea and sandwiches in her playhouse. I always had to sit in a child-sized white wicker chair.

On her first trip to Lancaster, Pennsylvania, when we bought the purple dress, we took her on a horse and buggy ride. The horse pooped many times during the forty-five-minute ride. When we returned home, she exclaimed to her grandparents that the horse did "number six." I have no idea why she said six instead of number two.

Grandma Bonnie—my mom—loved Leah to the moon and back. They did everything together from toddler to adult—shopping, cooking, watching TV, and outside work. I always found it amazing that my mom could get Leah to complete the same chores we asked her to do at our house. Just a side note, we live beside my parents so visits were always daily.

Grandma Bonnie and Pap Rick with their
beloved granddaughter

My grandmother had given us land to build a home beside my parents, so family was always close. Robin's parents were only thirty minutes away. Nana and Pap Higgins provided day trips and their usual unconditional love.

Leah with Pap Higgins on Leah's 15th birthday

Leah as a youngster loved to put curlers in my hair. One night when Robin was away, Leah had my hair doodled up with them when the doorbell rang. It was the Schwann delivery man. Thank goodness we were on a first name basis. I opened the door, and the look on his face was priceless.

As a little girl, Leah love to put hair ties and curlers in her dad's hair

Leah always loved school. She was an average B student. She was conscientious about her homework. In primary school we noticed her enthusiasm had waned. She cried on certain mornings. When I had a parent-teacher conference, I quickly realized the problem. She was afraid of her teacher. After talking with the teacher, I was livid. She said my daughter had displayed some mental retardation.

I got her removed from that class, and the new teacher greeted her with open arms. She went back to being her bubbly self and excelled the rest of the year. It was years later before I told Leah what happened at that conference. And on the night of her high school graduation when she received a stipend to attend college, I wanted to display a sign directed at the teacher, but I didn't. Other children, I found out, were subjected to the same ridicule, too, from that teacher who has since retired.

Leah was never overweight while in school. Yet, the start of peer pressure with a certain girl group she wanted to belong with started to rear its ugly head while she was in ninth grade. The school nurse called and said she was concerned about her loss of weight. She was focused on the prom and boys and had her eye on a certain dress.

The peer pressure didn't stop there. She had a group of friends who were middle class like herself. They came from good homes with parents who were accountable. She started experiencing drugs at age fifteen with marijuana. It took us awhile as parents to figure it out. I would wait up at night for her at the top of the steps. There were many late nights, and as she got older, it wound up being many sleepless nights.

At first she denied ever using or smoking marijuana, but the evidence was overwhelming. She finally conceded she was "just doing what my friends are doing." I always implored she be a leader, not a follower.

One night at the dinner table, she announced that she had gotten a job as a waiter at a local restaurant. We were astounded yet proud of her. She was never outgoing and we were perplexed about the choice of jobs. It seems peer pressure once again played a role. Some of her friends had gotten a job at the same establishment. Leah did well. She was so proud of herself, especially when she would come home and count her gratuity money.

She was saving money for a car. I taught her how to drive. We would go to the church parking lot with orange cones and empty water jugs. She would weave in and around them and parallel park. On the real highway, I would feel my toes coming through my running shoes, which at times felt like they were going through the floorboard of the small Kia. I was like any other dad experiencing nervousness. She did well on her driver's exam and was now on the road.

Leah also said she needed a companion. We were perplexed at what she meant. She was talking about a puppy. We were a pet-free home and weren't thrilled with that idea. Leah volunteered at the Humane Society and fell in love with "Pearl," but she was already adopted.

Enter the girl of our dreams: Iszabella. Leah named her, a beautiful Pekingese-Maltese mix bundle of joy from a local pet store. She was an early graduation gift from her Grandma Bonnie and Pap Rick. Iszygirl was so tiny that she couldn't navigate our steps, and we wondered for weeks if she would bark. She was easy to potty train, thanks to a bell on the front door. She loves people and adorns them with kisses when allowed. She would win "Best Kisser" at a local pet show and garnered the most votes as "Cutest" in a local newspaper contest—all within her first two years with us.

Leah with her new puppy Iszabella

I could devote an entire chapter to Iszabella because she means that much to our family. She is my mom's companion and spends her weekday mornings with her and most weekends. When Leah would return home from sober-living stints, Iszabella was always there to give her unconditional love. She has traveled with us on vacations and has visited Michigan, Ohio, Tennessee, North Carolina, South Carolina, Virginia, and many destinations throughout our home state of Pennsylvania.

After high school graduation, Leah started college at a nearby school. She majored in criminal justice. The first half year was great with dean's list grades. Then a boyfriend entered into the mix. Classroom attendance went down as did her grades. She was getting high and not going to school. Talk about a bad influence.

Her life then started spiraling out of control—bad acquaintances, former high school classmates who were different than the ones she had originally run around with, and a disregard for a vibrant lifestyle. She bounced around from house to house, instead of coming home.

When she did come home, she was in shambles. Arguing and physical confrontations were commonplace. We as parents were at our wits' end. We never experienced anything like this. What were we to do?

We prayed fervently for her to get her life back on track. There were glimmers of hope with two reenrollments back in college, only to be short-circuited by more drugs, the same bad acquaintances, and the same hellish path of destruction.

One Sunday night, she sat on the couch and said her life was "one screwed-up mess" and that she needed help. We reached out to a local detox/rehab facility. We spent the next morning getting her enrolled with a $14,000 price tag for two weeks of treatment. We thought this was the beginning to the end of her addiction.

Instead, it was the beginning of the beginning of her addiction.

She would relapse again. Next up, a three-hour trip to northern Pennsylvania to another facility where all staff were in recovery. This was a thirty-day program; then on to a nearby sober living home. It was during this journey at a Parents' Weekend program we met Robin and Sue from Allentown. Their son was going through the same program as Leah. We bonded and have been friends since that weekend.

Leah returned home and relapsed because she refused to give up her old acquaintances. She would delete them from her phone, only to put them back into her life.

To compound matters, she succumbed to peer pressure again when she joined a group of friends at a nearby gathering place along a creek. There was a tree rope they used to jump into the creek. She would never do this on her own, but she did this one Saturday afternoon. She hung onto the rope and didn't let go until she was alongside the rocky bank. She fell and crushed her right heel bone. Her foot swelled to the size of a small elephant's foot. No surgeon in the area would do the surgery. We took her to MedStar in Baltimore. The surgeon grafted bone from her knee to put into the heel, which was described as a crushed crouton. A few pins and a plate were inserted into the foot. Pain medication was prescribed. She ate them like Pez candy.

This time, she said, she was serious about getting clean. Instead of crutches, she navigated around on a knee walker. When her grandmother would take her shopping, it looked like she was qualifying for a NASCAR race as she raced up and down the aisles. An airplane aisle, however, was a different story.

Our friend Sue recommended that my wife call a sober solutions help hotline to find a rehab. They gave her information on elaborate rehab facilities in Florida that started at $30,000 a month. We wanted a place that would accept our $500 deductible insurance with no out-of-pocket expense. They directed us to a facility in Lake Arrowhead, California. My wife Robin wasn't about to let our daughter venture out to the West Coast on a knee walker by herself. Mother and daughter boarded the plane together and flew from Baltimore to Houston to Ontario, California. A terrible storm forced an overnight stay in Texas. Leah proclaimed that if her luggage was not at the California terminal when they arrived, she was turning around and heading home. The luggage was at the terminal.

From there, they endured a forty-five-minute rehab shuttle ride up the mountain with REO Speedwagon blasting: "I can't fight this feeling anymore." How appropriate.

At the clinic, the lady who greeted them said parents don't usually accompany their children.

Robin said: "I'm not like other parents. I needed to see the facility, where she was going and who she was going to be with… I wanted make sure this place was legitimate."

Ten minutes later, Robin was on her way down the mountain.

Leah did well at the rehab. She worked the program and was on her way to sobriety. Various sober living homes made pitches to her to come to their facility after she completed her stint at the rehab. Leah called and said two ladies came one day to talk about their sober living that was located two hours west in Los Angeles. She fell in love with this home. It would become her home on three different occasions. She excelled there because the owner, Amy, cared deeply for her. She had a sense of belonging, and they did everything as a group.

We visited her in Hollywood Hills at the sober living home. She was vibrant, flashing that pearly white smile and her disposition was calm and collected. We had conversation with her that included more than just yes or no answers. She was accepted for who she was, and she loved the group approach. Meetings, shopping, outings—they went together as a group.

We had our daughter back. Or so we believed. She would call almost every day to update us on her life. She would occasionally see celebrities at either the grocery store or at one of her nightly meetings. One call stunned us, however. She wanted to return to the East Coast. We were concerned about her sobriety because of the past acquaintances. We researched sober living homes and found one in Charlotte, North Carolina. Robin and I visited it and thought it would be ideal. We phoned Leah and described it. She was never fond of the South (except for the weather) because of the drive time. She agreed to make the move. We spent Christmas in Charlotte and moved her into the house the day after. It was a disaster. The room she was promised never became available. The job interview at the local restaurant never happened, and the guidance about public transportation never panned out by the housemates. She called and said she was being dropped off at a local hotel because of a physical confrontation with some of the residents.

We left right away for the six-hour trip. She had been sitting in the hotel lobby throughout the night and was a physical wreck. We left the Queen City without most of her belongings that were still at the sober living house, some of which were thrown in the front lawn by the residents. About half way home, her phone rang. It was the owner of the sober living home in California. She was checking in with Leah, making sure all was well. She didn't have a clue about what just happened. She told her to come "back home to California."

She did. And once again, Leah thrived.

We visited again. This time, we used it as a family vacation. Years before, we had visited San Diego and spent a week in Laguna Beach. She loved it. She was big fan of the TV series *The OC* and actually toured the school and many of the scenic places that were filmed for the show. This time around, we would go in the opposite direction, along the Pacific Coast Highway to Monterey Bay. It was a week filled with laughter, joy, and camaraderie. While in the grocery store, she asked if I ever had Mentos gum. I said no. Knowing that I've always been a gum chewer, she recommended I try it. I've been a Mentos fan ever since that day.

Vacationing in Laguna Beach—Robin and Leah enjoying chocolate covered strawberries

We thought she would stay at the sober living home. The owner of the home purchased another property and moved some of the ladies to that location. It was not a popular move for Leah because of the amount of steps. She was still rehabbing her heel. The owner asked her if she would be interested in becoming the assistant house manager. Leah had trepidation because of the duties and responsibilities, including driving a fifteen-passenger van in the busy streets of Los Angeles. Leah passed on the opportunity because she didn't have confidence in herself once again.

She then announced she was going to a sober living home in Minnesota. Minnesota? She had no idea how cold the winter would be. She called one Saturday morning and proclaimed that her new roommate told her to fully cover her face with a scarf because of frostbite and to completely dry her long beautiful hair because it would break off in the bitter cold conditions. Her stay was brief before she returned to the warm weather of California.

We thought this was the last of the moves, but because of expenses, she returned to the East Coast. She moved back home, and it resulted in going back to square one. She wanted to keep busy, so she volunteered at my place of employment—Fulton County Medical Center. That's where she met my coworkers, Wendy and Chris. She loved working at FCMC and was especially proud of wearing her ID badge. It was a sense of belonging. And she was a dedicated worker. She also got to drive for the first time in over four years. She would drive my pickup truck. It wasn't the fastest, and having to navigate the mountain to go to FCMC was good experience for her.

It was during this time that Leah and I would sit on the back deck of our home and talk—I mean really talk about life and things we hadn't shared in years. I told her that I was proud of her. She would get embarrassed. She would offset my positive with a negative about herself.

One evening during our many chats, I asked her if she had thought about her future. She said she took life one day at a time. I suggested that her future could include my parents' house. She put her head down, looked at me with tears in her eyes, and said, "Dad, I don't deserve their house after the hell I've put you all through with my life." I told her to look ahead and not in the rear view mirror.

A few weeks later, she came down downstairs to go onto the deck, but she stopped at the sliding glass door. I was sitting in the chair closest to the door and looked at her. She started to shake profusely. I had to pry her hands off the door handle. I yelled, "Leah, Leah!" I laid her down on the floor while I frantically called 911. The paramedics came and got her to respond. However, the response was not a good one. She ripped off all the electrodes they had placed on her. She was determined not to go to the ER. They took her anyway. We met her there, and she was contrite. The blood work and battery of tests came back negative. She denied any wrongdoing. I knew otherwise.

A week later, she confessed she was using synthetic marijuana. That was the result of the convulsions previously. Yet testing showed no ill effects. I alerted the hospital for future such cases.

It also meant another detox stint, this time in the Lancaster, Pennsylvania area. She also went to a sober living home in the city, and it was a dump in a downtrodden neighborhood where drugs were sold on the street, oftentimes in front of the sober living house. She then moved into a beautiful, but small, quaint sober living home in nearby Denver, Pennsylvania, with no public transportation. She would then move to a sister sober living home in Ephrata, Pennsylvania, one where public transportation was available.

While most of the sober living homes had an upside, none was better than the one she went back to several times in California. We often said it *was* her home away from home because the owner set the tone and the residents supported each other. There was no judgment. It was here that Leah met Jill, who to this day credits our daughter for helping her build a foundation to stay clean and sober. Many times, Jill wanted to leave and walk the streets of Los Angeles, but Leah wouldn't let her.

And for someone who didn't have confidence in herself, she found the inner strength to help others—the newcomers who would enter the sober living home. She would take them under her wing and show them the way and make them feel welcomed and at ease.

In 2006, we could have lost Leah, along with Robin and myself, to carbon monoxide poisoning. We had a cloudburst early one morning in mid-June that pounded us with over eleven inches of rain in over two hours. The water rushed across adjacent fields and into our side yard like white water swirling in a canyon. It caved in our basement door and ravaged our downstairs area. I had a sports den that was destroyed. We had many personal belongings that were floating in the four and a half feet of water in our basement. Outside, there was a car floating in our yard. The driver was taking a back road en route to Washington, DC, and was unaware of the flooded road because of the darkness of the morning. He hit the water and was trapped temporarily in his car. He managed to free himself from the floating car through his sunroof.

Meanwhile, we were scrambling in the dark to salvage at least some of our belongings from the basement. We had to rent pumps and hoses to eradicate the water. It would be a long process, with the pumps, fueled by gasoline, running around the clock for days. We had friends who helped us man the pumps, which needed refueled every hour. I was exhausted. We all were. Our friend Jeff volunteered to man the pumps while I tried to get a few hours of sleep on the first night of the flooding. I awoke at 10:00 p.m. and relieved him of his duties. I was still exhausted, but I knew I couldn't lay my head on the kitchen table. I felt lightheaded. As he left for home, he also mentioned of dizziness.

I made my way outside to the two pumps underneath our deck. I filled them with gasoline. When I turned around, I fell to the ground. I couldn't get back up. I belly crawled from under the deck across the yard to the garage door. I tried again to get up, but I was so dizzy and unable to stand. I continued to belly crawl inside the garage to the kitchen door. Robin and Leah were both sleeping upstairs. I knew something was terribly wrong. I tried standing again, only to get to my knees. I opened the door and yelled numerous times to get out of the house.

Leah heard my voice and awakened her mom. They ran down to find me yelling in the doorway to get out of the house—something was wrong. Robin went back upstairs to change out of her bedclothes. When she returned, she tried to help me out of the garage. I fell unconscious on the garage floor. Robin said she immediately called 911. Her cellphone just happened to be turned on and in her coat pocket. I had vomited and quit breathing. The 911 dispatch operator asked Robin what was going on. She said I had vomited. He instructed her on how to clear my airway. It worked. I was breathing again. The EMS crew arrived and evaluated all of us. Both Robin and Leah felt dizzy. I was admitted to ICU. I woke up with tubes and hoses hooked up to me. I suffered from carbon monoxide poisoning. My level was 23. The fatal number is 25. I was in the hospital for five days. They were both treated and released. Our home was filled with carbon monoxide, according to the fire department. Despite the pumps being outside, the fumes were circulating inside the basement and got into our heating and cooling system, which circulated it throughout our home. We had to stay with my parents for a week until the system was rechecked and deemed safe.

Meanwhile, our friends showed up for several days to help clean the basement by discarding the rubbage and power washing everything in sight. When Robin was bringing me home from the hospital, I said we had a long road ahead of us because of the cleanup ahead. She looked at me, smiled, and said I should focus on a full recovery and that we shouldn't worry because our "cleaning angels" were taking care of it.

I knew I had a lot of angels taking care of me over that weeklong nightmare.

CHAPTER 6

Love from Above

When I first met Kevin Simmers on February 16, 2018—two days after Leah's passing—I was impressed with his compassion. He hugged me before he said a word. And then he sat and listened. There were no interruptions on his part. He listened intently. And then he spoke. He had entered into this fraternity in 2015 when his daughter Brooke overdosed on heroin.

He is not one to mince words. I guess his career as a police officer taught him that. But on this day, he spoke with and of compassion. He shared Brooke's story and how he cries almost every day. He talked about that grief as if it were a noose around his neck and that we would most likely find it most difficult to break free from it, too. He made that assessment based on how he gauged our love for Leah and the brokenness he saw in us from the previous sixty minutes. And he shared scientific information he had learned regarding an addict's brain and how it functions. In ninety minutes, I knew we had an ally; we had a friend.

And then when only I asked did he talk about Brooke's House. Kevin promised his daughter a sober living house unlike the ones she had stayed in, if she remained drug-free for one year. Tragically, she died on April 14, 2015. The promise was kept, however, in loving memory and to keep the nineteen-year-old's legacy alive. Three months after her death, the Simmers family started the journey of fulfilling Brooke's dream by creating Brooke's House.

The Brooke's House Story

With the guidance of family friends Kathy Hall and Jeff Bohn, both professionals familiar with non-profit organizations, Brooke's House earned its status as a non-profit entity. With its 501(c)3 designation, all donations would be tax-free for the donor. After looking at residential properties throughout Hagerstown, Kevin drove to Technology Boulevard to look at a parcel of land that was free of other homes and serene, apart from the hustle and bustle of downtown Hagerstown.

The land was owned by the Fulton family. On the day Kevin looked at the property, a double rainbow appeared over the property. It was a sign of great things to come, as Adna Fulton and his family donated the 3.5 acres and a plan was put into place to build Brooke's House. Jason Divelbiss, who was a source of inspiration for the project and encouraged Kevin and Dana many times over to move forward with it, helped transfer the property to the newly-approved non-profit organization.

Starting from scratch, they could design Brooke's House to include everything many typical sober living homes didn't have—nice bedrooms, a kitchen with ample room, a chapel, a common room that wasn't cramped or used as a secondary bedroom. The Simmers family was blessed to have the late Dave Rider apply his talents as the contractor. Rider stepped forward on Day One and didn't look back, making sure Brooke's House was constructed in a timely fashion with superior craftsmanship. He promised the family he would do whatever it took to make the house a reality. He would pass soon after Brooke's House opened its doors on July 8, 2019.

But they needed funds to make it happen.

Brooke's death didn't go under the radar as Kevin, a former narcotics detective in Hagerstown, spoke at local schools about his daughter's tragic passing and the drug epidemic that is prevalent in his own community. It led to civic organizations and churches inviting him to share "Brooke's Story." They financially supported his efforts by making donations to Brooke's House. Soon, media outlets began picking up the story. Local media coverage turned into regional interviews that turned into national coverage. Outlets in Washington aired his poignant story. Then came NPR, Fox News, BBC Worldwide. Donations would come from all over the world after each interview.

The community embraced the facility as well—from a place to build, to members who fill the board of directors, and business partners in the community who were willing to give of their time, treasure and talents. Groundbreaking was held May 1, 2018.

[Kevin shared:] "For many of the volunteers, it's personal—many of them have lost a loved one to a drug overdose. It's a way for them to give back. Dana and I know about the pain, grief, anger and suffering that others are experiencing because we still have those moments, too. There are really no words of consolation for someone who loses a loved one they cared for and loved so much. However, they can feel at ease to tell their story and talk with us because we are open, honest, transparent and nonjudgmental, which helps everyone. For many, helping with Brooke's House is way to stay positive. We suggest to people, find something that inspires them, something they believe in and support wholeheartedly. Stay positive and have faith in God, who is in control."

I asked Kevin if he had literature on the Brooke's House project. He reluctantly went to his car and handed me a brochure. I also noticed he had a set of blueprints in his back seat for a meeting later that day. I asked if I could see them.

From that gathering, Robin and I knew we wanted to support the Brooke's House project in memory of Leah. My mom and dad wanted to help, too.

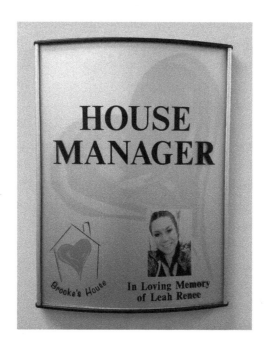

So we named the house manager's room in Leah's memory and was able to decorate it in the things that Leah loved. Robin customized a large Hello Kitty wall decal to bear Leah's favorite colors: purple and leopard print with the words *Leah's Room*. The bedspread is leopard print. There are elephant figurines and a plaque displayed in her memory. Diane, the house manager at the time, loved her room.

The Straley Family presenting Kevin Simmers
(between Mike and Robin) with a named gift to
Brooke's House in memory of Leah

Leah's room lovingly decorated by Leah's mother and grandmother at Brooke's House

Robin got involved with the main social enterprise at Brooke's House: Brooke's House Chocolate. Prior to Brooke's House opening, a group of volunteers came together to make chocolate as part of the fundraising needs. Once residents were in the house, they would lead the chocolate-making enterprise to help encourage and inspire change while building character and strength to achieve happiness and hope for a new tomorrow. By making chocolates, Brooke's House created an avenue of independent, self-supporting revenue for the home while residents learned a new and exciting skill in making delicious chocolate delicacies.

Brooke's House online chocolate orders available at
www.brookeshousechocolate.org
Photo courtesy of Kevin G. Gilbert

Mike making nonpareils at Brooke's House

The business concept of making chocolates for profit was created when Mike Griffin from Cape Cod saw an interview of Kevin on Martha MacCallum's show *The Story* on Fox News.

So on many fall weekends and weeknights in 2018, Robin busily helped produce, package, promote, and deliver Brooke's House Chocolate. She reached out to high school classmates, coworkers, and business associates who all excitedly agreed to volunteer. It was grief support for Robin, who wanted to stay busy and channel her brokenness into something positive. It wasn't so much just the chocolate making but the camaraderie that she found therapeutic.

I stayed at home and grieved.

She encouraged me to get involved. I reluctantly did so with the chocolate making and was engulfed with the same type of purposeful belonging. For those hours of fulfillment provided a Band-Aid of comfort.

Robin would later join the board of directors at Brooke's House and redesigned both the Brooke's House and Brooke's House Chocolate websites.

I helped write copy for each, took chocolate to work to sell, and invited the Fulton County Medical Center Foundation Board of Directors to hold our monthly meeting at the House in March of 2019. They knew Robin and I were involved with Brooke's House and always asked for updates. What better way to give them an update, I thought, than to invite them to tour the beautiful facility. They were impressed. And Kevin made them feel welcomed. The FCMC Foundation Board, on our behalf, contributed $1,780 toward the furniture for the room named in Leah's memory.

Soon the chocolate-making volunteers were assisted by the first residents of Brooke's House. Robin came home one night and said I needed to volunteer the next weekend so I could meet them.

Nichole, Stacey, Mandy, Cara, Marybeth, Robin, Iantha, and Diane.

They melted my heart.

They all looked me in the eye and gave me a warm hug. They all wore green shirts. As newbies at Brooke's House, residents are given a green shirt to wear in their first thirty days.

Robin is called "Miss Robin." I'm called "Mr. Mike," except for Stacey who refers to me as "Uncle Fred" because I look like her relative.

We prepared two meals for them, the first when we did a Leah Legacy bag distribution (more about that in chapter 7) in late summer of 2019 and then again around Christmas in 2019.

Every time I'm around the ladies at Brooke's House, I'm filled with joy. They make me smile and feel alive. My broken heart is temporarily mended.

Robin says every hug given or received is like that from Leah.

My mom loves Brooke's House, but staggers her visits because it's a reminder of what could've been for her granddaughter. This sober living home is unlike any others we've ever visited.

And for that, we give thanks to God for leading and directing Kevin Simmers in fulfilling his daughter's wish.

www.brookeshouse.org

CHAPTER 7

Be a Voice

Three days after Leah's memorial service, we attended Sunday morning worship service at Covenant Life Church where we held the Thursday night memorial gathering.

We were greeted by so many parishioners who offered their condolences. Pastor Tim's message focused on *worry*, which is the enemy of faith and worship. Halfway through the service a hand came across my back left shoulder. In it was a prayer request card. On this card were these words: "Be a voice. God loves you and is with you."

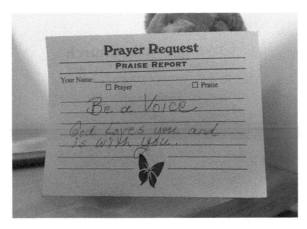

My handkerchief was already saturated from the tears shed throughout the morning. I turned around to see who had given me these words of encouragement. It was Linda, who normally sits in the pew behind us. She was looking right at me with her beautiful smile and nodded with a wink. After service, she said she was inspired to give me these words because she knew I would use them.

I kept that card, displaying it in our walk-in closet. Every morning, I would read the card. Every night, I would read the card. I prayed about the words.

Days and weeks passed. A season passed, and another. Early fall was upon us, and on my way home from work one pleasant evening, a voice spoke inside me: *Recreate the bag. Recreate the bag*, it repeated. I pulled over and gathered myself. What am I supposed to do?

And then it became clear.

When Leah was at the sober living home in Ephrata, Pennsylvania, a church group had visited them in early December of 2017. They came bearing gifts, which were beautifully wrapped—except one. Leah took the one that was in a garbage bag. In it was a handbag with many compartments that held assorted gift cards and an abundance of essentials like toiletry items, a journal, word find books, and assorted stationary items. A winter scarf and glove set and umbrella were also included. She called home that Sunday and was excited. It was one big run-on sentence. She didn't stop for periods with her sentences.

Now, we needed to recreate the bag and serve others like she had been served. We would call it a Leah Legacy bag, only it would be a purple reusable drawstring bag. We chose purple because it was Leah's favorite color and it's also the color for overdose awareness. As for the bag, we weren't using a garbage bag. We wanted the recipients to be able to reuse the bag for their many meetings and appointments, while drawing attention to the Leah Legacy logo.

When I shared with Robin the idea and concept, we both immediately sat down and created a list of items that would go into the bag. We harkened back to the conversation we had with Leah and then added to it. Over thirty items were jotted down. We had the idea. We had the logo. We didn't have items or any funding. We needed to buy these items in bulk to make all the bags the same.

We cobbled together a letter and sent it to our friends and relatives. They responded overwhelmingly. Donations of $10, $25, and $100 came our way. They gave a total of $1,600 in a little over a month. Barb at FastInk—a local promotions company—donated the first imprinted one hundred drawstring bags. Robin ordered product from several different vendors. Canteen Vending donated assorted snacks for the bags. Bombas approved an in-kind gift of 1,000 pair of socks.

Here's what is in each Leah Legacy bag:

- Bombas® socks
- Toothbrush
- Toothbrush cover
- Toothpaste
- Dental floss
- Adult coloring book
- Puzzle book
- Notebook

- Ink pen
- Coloring pencils
- Pencil sharpener
- Wet® hairbrush
- Comb
- Lip balm
- Deodorant
- Manicure set
- Bath/shower sponge
- Bath towel
- Pocket tissue packs
- Snacks: pretzels, peanuts, trail mix, crackers

Seasonal Items

- Umbrella
- Winter hat, gloves, and scarf
- Throw blanket
- Hand cream
- Sunblock

Our first distribution was at the sober living home in Ephrata where Leah received that garbage bag. It was planned that way. It was one year after Leah had received hers. The ladies greeted us with open arms. The owner and her dad were there to help us carry in all the bags. We also had gloves, hats, and scarves they could choose from a large box, with various colors and styles.

Our first distribution of Leah's Legacy bags to Grace House

One young lady said it was the first time in over a month she had deodorant. Another lady said she needed the hairbrush.

This was repeated time and time again when we did distributions. When women go into a sober living home, oftentimes they don't have a lot of personal belongings. Some just have what they are wearing. They are grateful for the Leah Legacy bag and for the compassion that's centered around it.

We shared Leah's story of addiction, which many already knew from being at that house. Then we shared our story as grieving parents. We emphasized the love we had for our daughter and the rocky journey we all experienced. We also shared our love and hope for each of the residents. When it was time for a group photo, I noticed a beautiful photo of Leah on the side of the refrigerator. It brought tears to my eyes. Grace, the owner, said Leah was and always will be loved. And the photo will always be there.

Robin and I shed tears of joy.

Now, it was on to the next distribution: Frederick, Maryland, then another in Hagerstown, Maryland. There, we distributed and shared with fifty residents. Fifty hugs felt really good that morning. Then more of the same at Brooke's House.

Wakefield House distribution

Lasting Change distribution

Brooke's House distribution

Pastor Tim asked us to share our story and mission with the Covenant Life Church congregation. We did. They responded with an offering of $1,040. Each bag costs about $50. Twenty more bags were going to be distributed as a result of their generosity.

More tears. More joy.

Our actions were spurred on by those words of encouragement—*be a voice*—from that note card written by a beautiful person who followed her heart.

I believe I speak for many parents when I say that we must not be silent. If we are to begin to heal as a society, we must dispel stigma by coming forward and sharing our stories. By doing so, we can make substance use disorder part of everyday conversation without the fear of judgment or shame.

I ask, please be mindful of negative things that might be thought or said about "drug addicts." If they aren't empathetic and kind words, then perhaps just listen. I learned that lesson from my parents: "If you can't say something nice, then don't say anything at all."

Listen to the fact that we are all at risk for addiction, a brain chemistry disease that is not controlled by willpower.

CHAPTER 8

Leah's Legacy Foundation

With more distributions in late 2018 and into the early parts of 2019, we were getting financial gifts to help buy the items that were going into the Leah Legacy bags.

Since I serve as the executive director of the Fulton County Medical Center Foundation, I thought it would be wise to create our own foundation. We were in this outreach for the long term; and if we wanted to apply for grants, sponsorships, and other external funding, we needed to be a 501(c)(3) nonprofit. It also allowed more people to give a tax-deductible gift.

On the advice of our financial advisor, I reached out to a local firm to help us prepare the official paperwork for the nonprofit status. I spoke to the principal owner. He was taken back by our actions after hearing about the tragedy. He did the work pro bono. We are grateful. We also had to establish a set of bylaws, along with policies and procedures. We worked with a local law office. They discounted their work for us.

We submitted the paperwork on May 15, 2019, and were surprised to receive our official notification letter from the state on June 12, 2019.

Leah's Legacy was an official nonprofit.

I discussed with Robin the need for a Facebook page and a website. My wife is very creative. She created the pages with the necessary headers and artwork. I wrote the copy. She put it all together as you see it today.

The Facebook page is Leah's Legacy. The website is www.leahslegacy.net.

In the summer of 2019, our Franklin County chapter of GRASP (Grief Recovery After Substance Passing) met at our home to assist us with packing product into fifty Leah Legacy Bags. It was a time to fellowship, while doing a good deed. Typically, we meet at a church and tearfully share each other's stories and grief. This night was marked with pizza, laughter, smiles, and heartfelt hugs. Then I flagged down an unsuspected driver on our country road to ask if they would take a group photo of us. That was fun.

Our friends from the local GRASP chapter gathered
to assemble Leah's Legacy bags

In creating the Leah's Legacy Foundation, we needed board members to satisfy our bylaw requirements. We asked our pastor, Tim Fisher, to serve as president. We asked our newly made friend Amanda Staley from our local chapter of GRASP to join us. And we asked longtime friend Denise Timmons, who dearly loved Leah, to be the secretary. All wholeheartedly agreed. Robin serves as the treasurer. I am the founder. We meet quarterly with a detailed agenda and an action plan to keep the momentum going with funding for product and marketing for awareness.

A few nights a week, Robin and I work on the necessities of keeping Leah's Legacy Foundation going. Follow-up thank you cards with handwritten messages, contacting folks for speaking engagements, product donations and Leah Legacy bag distributions, completing grant applications, and delving into fundraising opportunities are just some of the things that keep us busy.

Once we gained nonprofit status, we put together a list of small companies who we were going to ask to donate product. They ranged from a Wet hairbrush company to beauty manufacturers. The Wet hairbrush company marketing lady said they would be honored to help us. The same can be said for Bombas socks. They donated 1,000 pairs of socks. When you hear them say their mission hasn't changed—one pair purchased is equal to one pair donated—believe them.

Robin's high school classmate friends have been instrumental in helping us. From individual donations, volunteering, and helping us fundraise, they have cared and supported us from the outset. We had a fundraiser late in the summer in 2019 at a restaurant that is owned by a twenty-something young man, whose Uncle Kevin is a classmate. We had a packed house at his establishment that netted us $700. Another classmate, Mary Ellen, an Avon representative, established a highly discounted program on shower gel and lip balm that people could purchase and donate to our cause—435 of these items were purchased.

We received a grant from Franklin-Fulton Drug & Alcohol in the fourth quarter of 2019 for $6,500 to help us reach more women in need. Those monies set in motion monthly distributions at PA Counseling and Pyramid Counseling, along with the two sober living homes. We received an additional $2,000 grant from WellSpan Health in the summer of 2020.

Moreover, we also took a stab at securing a large donation from a prominent consumer product company that set up its largest warehouse distribution center in a neighboring state. One of Robin's coworkers had a contact and shared our request letter with the human resources manager. He was interested in helping us, he told Michelle, Robin's coworker, back on September 18 of 2019; but it would take time. He sent Robin a text message on January 8, 2020, to set up the time and date for us to pick up product. On January 16, 2020, she drove her car, and I drove our pickup truck with the eight-foot bed.

What an experience we had at the distribution center. First, the air was filled with an aroma of a popular dryer sheet as we met Ryan, our point person and the gentleman responsible for making this donation happen. Then we waited in line at the truck entrance for clearance. We were the only ones not in an 18-wheeler. Then for the donation itself, a pallet of shampoos and conditioners (546 bottles of shampoos, 486 bottles of conditioners) were loaded onto the truck bed. A second pallet, yes a second pallet, had to be broken down and stacked inside the truck bed around the other pallet. Product included 72 packages of sanitary napkins, 24 rolls of paper towels, 8 packets of toilet paper (12 pack), 12 cans of air freshener, 12 large bottles of body wash, 10 large containers of dish detergent, 17 large bottles of house cleaner and disinfectant, 30 boxes of dryer sheets, 12 boxes of sweeper refills, 30 brand name dusters, 18 packages of dental floss, 23 razor refill cartridges, and another 144 brand name razor refill cartridges.

Ryan (far right) was instrumental in providing Leah's Legacy Foundation with inventory
of toiletries and cleaning supplies for sober living homes and residents

The truck bed and cab were filled as was the car's backseat and trunk. What a donation. Dollar value was estimated to be around $5,000, according to Ryan.

Wow!

As we drove separately home, it dawned on me where and how are we going to unload this wonderful donation.

We pulled the truck into the garage that Thursday night. My mom said we could store the product at her home (remember, we live beside each other) in a basement room. This kept the products safe from freezing. We certainly didn't have room at our home. We already had items pigeonholed in upstairs closets, in the garage, and in an outside utility shed.

So now that we had a home for the product, how do we unload it? Robin put out feelers to our board, past volunteers and friends for that Saturday morning. We were going to form a human chain from the out-side basement doors to the laundry room storage area. Within forty-five minutes, we had eleven volunteers lined up. That Saturday morning, we had everything unloaded and safely stored within forty-five minutes.

Friends help unload and store two skids of donated supplies

It led to me thinking about a designated building—we would name it Leah's Legacy Operations Center—where all product would be stored and our packing and storage of bags would be housed. We would fundraise for this building, a small yet comfortable outpost that would take us from doing everything in our garage to a more comfortable setting. We would build it on mom and dad's property, adjacent to another storage building.

We would need $16,000. We received a $5,000 grant from a very generous family foundation, another $2,000 from an energy company grant, a $2,000 donation from my parents that would be matched by another $1,000 from my mom's employer, and another $1,000 came from a community bank outside of our county. COVID-19 hit just as we were about to start the letter campaign portion of the fundraising campaign. We had to wait for almost two months before we resumed our donor asks. A Facebook post asking for donations on my fifty-seventh birthday generated $1,057. We exceeded our goal of $16,000.

The electric was donated by Robin's cousin, Bo. The inside finishing work was donated by our friend Jerry from GRASP. Some of the signage was donated by my good friend Jay who owns a sign company. The gutter and spouting work was donated by a co-worker's husband and his company. The insulation, drywall, drop ceiling, and inside trim were donated by Robin's classmate, who owns a construction company. The inside painting was donated by a friend who is a professional painter. The beautiful flooring was discounted by a business colleague of Robin's. The attractive landscaping complete with the stone walkway was discounted by a local landscaper who we've done business with for years. We held an Open House in October of 2020. Nearly 125 guests—those who have assisted us with donations, monetarily and/or in-kind goods/services, through this journey—attended the event. They experienced building a "Leah Legacy Bag" and what goes into each bag that we distribute, along with walking through Leahbug's Memorial Garden. It was a night to behold. We are blessed.

Leahbug's garden created by Leah's mom and grandmother

We are blessed to have so many rally around our cause.

I can't imagine what Leah would say about these efforts. From a foundation named in her memory to a building constructed and dedicated in her name.

I do know our love for her is just as strong today as it was when she was alive. And I do know our efforts aren't in vain, and I do know we are grateful for each and every donation and the support we receive to bring necessities, cheer, and love to women who are recovering from addiction.

Pictures of Leah's Legacy Operations Center

Open House of Leah's Legacy Operations Center

CHAPTER 9

What's Next

We've been asked, "What's next? What's the next chapter with Leah's Legacy Foundation?"

Only God knows what He wants us to do. I will follow His lead. Robin and I do have some ideas. We would like to create a sober living home for women, much like Brooke's House, only ours would be called "Leah's Home." Our hopes would be to have an existing home that we could transform into a sober living home.

The need is great in every community, and ours is no different. We live in a rural community on the country roads where the smell of freshly cut hay permeates your nasal passages on any late spring or summer evening.

We also would like to expand our distribution of Leah Legacy bags to more sober living homes and group counseling settings.

We need to let people know about our foundation, from a fiscal standpoint so we can constantly have streams of revenue to assist with the program and from a view so we can accomplish our mission to provide necessities, cheer, and love to women in sober-living environments.

I want to speak to people—groups of people—from school assemblies to people in recovery to grieving parents. Small or large, it makes no difference to me. I will travel to share Leah's story, our story as parents. Morning or night, I want to share what Robin and I are doing. I want to share this book. I want to listen to parents who carry the same burden we carry. I want to share their tears. I want to give them a heartfelt hug. I have a message, and I want to share it with the masses. I'm not a great orator, but I have experience in public speaking. I let my heart carry the message. It is, after all, the heart that has the hole and needs mending.

Call me crazy, but Leah and I shared a special bond as a father-daughter during her baby-infant-toddler years. When I would walk or rock her to sleep, I would sing a song about a fictional bird. I would make up rhymes about this colorful bird. I have always wanted to make this bird come alive, if you will, by creating it through a stuffed toy, a coloring book, and an illustrated story book (I know, another book). The proceeds would go back into Leah's Legacy Foundation. My vision is to connect with a Christian musical group or musician who would be interested in selling these items at their concerts. I would also make them available on our website and at my speaking engagements.

Our daughter's passing is still difficult to comprehend, and the grief is still thick. We forge along each day, putting one foot in front of the other, hoping each passing hour will be better than the previous one. I read the daily posts on the GRASP-protected Facebook page, and tears well up in my eyes. I serve on several local task force committees, and I hear the horror stories about the opioid addiction in our community, neighboring communities, county, state, and region. Sometimes, I want to walk out of the room and vomit because I know the heartbreak that's going on inside these families, or about to happen. Some care more than others. When we held our overdose awareness events or when we talk to women in recovery, the gamut of emotions from the parents and those who are trying to get their lives back on track are piercing. Some of the comments are rather cold and hard: "I wish she would just die." Some are from a hurting heart: "My parents have given up on me." Some are out of frustration: "I simply don't know which way to turn. I have tried to help her, and nothing seems to be working."

Robin and I are on the road to recovery, not from an addiction, but from experiencing the loss of our daughter. We will never fully recover, but we want to offer hope and love to the millions of grieving parents and women in addiction.

It is what Leah Renee Straley would want us to do.

Fields of Happiness and Pain

Robin R. Straley

Sunflowers represent happiness.

That's how I always viewed sunflowers—as being big happy smiling faces standing tall and at attention drinking in the warmth of the summer sun. When photos start showing up on Facebook as the end of summer nears, everyone's excitement comes alive asking those who have posts "Where are the fields?" Plans need to be made quickly with loved ones and family because in a matter of weeks the huge local field flowing with rich yellow happiness will turn into a not-so-happy, dried-up, dreary field.

Mike and I recently made a trip to Clemson University to see our beloved Tigers play a game of football. While driving around campus exploring where our game day parking pass would be, we noticed fields of sunflowers in full bloom. We pulled over to figure out which road would lead to the dirt road that would lead to happiness—or so we thought.

You see our last visit to the field of happiness was when Leah was alive.

We saw the Facebook posts by our friends, and so we asked, "Where are the fields?" We made our plans with Leah and her grandmother because we had very little time to get to these flowing yellow fields of happiness to snap our perfect photos.

Our planned Saturday finally came. Our excitement was building. We searched high and low for that field of happiness only to return home unhappy and no family photos to post. We sought out happiness the next day, a Sunday afternoon, driving on back roads asking folks who were outside, "Where are the sunflower fields?" Finally, after turning onto a small, narrow road, cresting over a hill, they were in the distance—our field of happiness.

We sought out our perfect spot to take our perfect family photos. It was a fun time deciding who was going to pose together with who and how. We were finally there, relishing the moments that everyone else had experienced. Our little bit of happiness now recorded on images that will last a lifetime. A lifetime. A lifetime, though, without one family member: Leah.

So we made our way to the sunflower field in Clemson to take selfies to post of us with the flowers that are known to represent happiness. It started off well, but the longer we stayed the quick lightning speed of a trigger came with Mike doubling over from the agony and painful memories of when we once stood in a flowing yellow field of happiness and Leah in the middle of it. We had to get out, quickly.

If you look closely at a fully grown sunflower, it almost appears that its face is bowing down from the weight of the seeds that are growing in it. Grief is the same way. It makes you stand a little less tall and bow over from the weight of that pain and tragedy of that loss.

Living with grief and the loss of our daughter has been the most painful journey of our lives. Yes, it comes and goes. Yes, some days are better than others; but we are not able to do what used to be—holiday celebrations and family gatherings, baking favorite cookies, going to favorite restaurants, fixing favorite foods, or going Christmas shopping. All those past loving acts of happiness are now triggers that come at us at lightning speed, forcing us to bow over in pain from remembering the days when we once had holiday celebrations and family gatherings with Leah, baked Leah's favorite cookies, invited Leah to come along to our favorite restaurants, fixed Leah's favorite foods, or asked, "Leah, what would you like for Christmas?"

Everything has to be done differently to get through the life we now live.

Our memories are now etched in time and in our minds as sorrowful recalls of what was and what will never be again. Every day is filled with Leah.

Blog dated Oct. 1, 2019

CHAPTER 10

Agape Love

The ancient Greeks had four words for love. The first is *philia*, the affection that grows from friendship. The second is *storge*, the kind you have for a sibling. The third is *eros*, the uncontrollable urge to say "I love you." The fourth kind of love is different, the most admirable. It's called *agape*—love that takes action. It takes courage, strength, and sacrifice.

The first three describe the different kinds of love that people feel. The fourth—agape—is selfless love. It's what has inspired Robin and I to do for the women who are determined to overcome their addiction and live healthy, vibrant lives.

We desperately wanted that for Leah.

And so did she.

For those who have gone down the same path as many of us have, you know all the feelings—frustration, anger, and helplessness, to just name a few, in the struggles. You also know the joy, love, and compassion in the smallest victories.

It has been mentioned already, but it's worth repeating: we tried to fix Leah. There is no fixing. It has to start and end with the individual who is struggling. They must have the *want to* to fix themselves.

For me and especially Robin, although we wavered at times, there was always Agape love.

Let's look more closely at what makes up this kind of love and how we applied each:

Action. Driving her to appointments, doing trial runs on public transportation, traveling with her to California to make sure she arrived safely at the treatment facility, being part of the many phone conversions in a three-way conference call to ensure her finances, schooling and treatment appointments were properly done, etc.

Courage. Saying no, being persistent and persuasive, being accountable, and setting a good example

Strength. Knowing our limitations and recognizing we couldn't do it all, although at times we wanted to. We also needed each other to work with each other because addicts, much like children, will try to divide and conquer.

Sacrifice. God knows our hearts, and He knows what we went through, especially financially. He has provided in so many ways, including giving me parents who always were willing to assist us in whatever financial situation arose through Leah's addiction. There were vacations and events that were either cut short or cancelled because of the circumstances that came with her struggles.

Yet, we *always* stood by her. It wasn't always easy, but we knew her as our daughter with a lovable personality, not the person who had an addiction that could bring out a disposition unbecoming to her and those she loved.

Agape love is why Robin and I stood by Leah.

Agape love is why we grieve every day and continue to do so.

Agape love is why Robin was so persistent with the detectives.

Agape love is why we sent a letter to our friends asking them to support us in buying supplies to put into a purple bag.

Agape love is why we share Leah's story and our story as parents when we do a Leah Legacy bag distribution.

Agape love is why we created the Leah Legacy Foundation.

Agape love is why we built the Leah Legacy Operations Center from donations.

Agape love is why we will continue to expand our reach into other areas of sobriety for women.

Agape love is what inspires Robin and me to put others' needs before our own.

Agape love is always loving our daughter, Leah Renee Straley, forever twenty-six, who has provided us with the action, courage, strength, and sacrifice to do the right thing, be our best, and help build better futures for women who want to live drug-free and productive lives.

Our Last Christmas with Leah

Love Notes

Robin R. Straley

I remember, back in the day a long, long time ago when Mike and I were dating, how he would leave a torn piece of paper from his reporter's notebook taped to the steering wheel of my car; and on it were precious words of love of his feelings for me. As soon as I would get in my car, there it was. A little love note to cling to until the next time we were together.

On one evening, six months later, he took me to a local roller skating rink parking lot to propose. Why a roller rink? Well, this roller rink represented a most humiliating date because I could roller skate but Mike could not. He clung to the walls until he made one complete lap and took off his roller skates for good. Never again. In remembrance of that date, he decided to take me back to that location to ask me the big question, placing a make shift rubber band bracelet on my arm with a piece of torn paper inscribed with *sold* on it. Of course, I said yes. That paper rubber band bracelet has been stored safely in our lock box ever since.

Throughout our thirty-three years of marriage, he would continue to drop "love notes" to me, especially when he was going out of town for a business trip. In all this time, I cannot remember one time he failed to leave me a note. All of those notes of love were so precious to me, and after so many years of being together, his feelings have never changed.

Mike now writes love notes to Leah—nightly.

My eyes can't help but well up with tears when I think of his devotion and the painstaking love he sends to Leah each night. He writes to her before going to sleep. One love note every night since she died on Valentine's Day 2018.

All those love notes are written in a small Clemson Tigers journal that sits on our dresser. He's filled up three journals so far.

More often than not, I hear his cries of love as he writes to our daughter. Brokenhearted with the loss of twenty-six years of memories. Every day is filled with Leah.

I've never asked Mike what he writes to Leah each night, nor have I tried to look at the sentiments that are written in those three personal journals. The one thing I do know is that each word and each sentence penciled on paper of each nightly love note are loving tributes and promises by a very special and loving father to his only daughter that will continue until they see each other again one day.

Blog dated February 13, 2020

ABOUT THE AUTHOR

Michael L. Straley is like so many other parents who have lost a child to a drug overdose. He grieves every day. His life has been forever changed since that fateful call on Valentine's morning 2018.

With a burning desire to help others who are on the road to recovery, he is using his journalistic and fund-raising skills to team with his wife, Robin, to create the Leah's Legacy Foundation, a nonprofit established in 2019 in memory of their beloved daughter, Leah Renee.

Straley earned his communication-journalism degree from Shippensburg University and his master's in Integrated Marketing Communications from Eastern Michigan University. A former newspaper journalist who then became a communications/marketing/fundraising executive, he and Robin share Leah's story of addiction and theirs as grieving parents to women in recovery and with parents who are struggling over the loss of a loved one. Their candid stories and the presentation of a purple Leah's Legacy bag help with the healing process. It's their way of providing necessities, cheer, and love to those who are in a sober-living environment.

Photo courtesy of Kevin G. Gilbert